LET

THE HOUSE OF AARON

SAY

Book One

of the "Series of Seven" Collection

CAROL SCHEITLIN

New Life Expressions

Publishing Division

LET THE HOUSE OF AARON SAY

Published by New Life Expressions, Publishing Division, in the United States of America.

ISBN: 978-1-7320538-0-9 (Paperback)

Scripture quotations are taken from the Authorized King James Version (public domain). Bold text, italics, underline, or parenthetical comments within Scripture quotations indicate emphasis added by the author.

Cover design and setup by Dawn Papandrea-Sherrod. www.DPK-GraphicDesign.com

Printed in the United States of America

2018 – First Edition

DEDICATION

Dedicated with great thanks to God Who divinely orchestrates all details of our lives for His glory. Knowing God's sovereignty in all things, I dedicate this respectfully also to my Jewish friends, and their families and the generations of their families to come. To my beloved family. To my beloved co-workers and their families. To precious friends who have stuck with me through all seasons of life. To Joanne, who taught me and taught many the beauty, and joy of worshiping God through Hebrew dance. To Ann, thankful for our Divine appointment at Ocean Grove. And thankful also to John & Michelle, in appreciation for a life-changing event on a special Sunday evening in 2017 at the Great Auditorium. I'm so very thankful also to the beloved Jewish people, the chosen of God, from Whom our Mashiach/Messiah comes, *exactly* as prophecy foretells. And finally, all dedicated to my Beloved of all beloveds, the King of kings, my Savior and Redeemer - the God of Abraham, Isaac, and Jacob - for His glory always.

ACKNOWLEDGMENTS

Thankful for those who have offered their prayers, talents, skills and wisdom to prep this work for print, including precious friend Val, Yosef, and incredibly talented graphic designer Dawn Papandrea-Sherrod (DPK Graphic Design).

LET

THE HOUSE OF AARON

SAY

TABLE OF CONTENTS

INTRODUCTION

Dear Reader,

This is the beginning of a journey. It is one of a series of books that may be among the most important you have ever read up to this point in your life. This book contains words of life from the Giver of all life. Its purpose is to glorify G-d, the Creator of all things, the very One Who brought you into existence.

You have been placed in this world for a distinct purpose, and positioned at this unique time in all history. The fact that you are alive today is proof that your mission here on earth is not yet completed.

It is my hope and prayer that because you have picked up this book to read, that you may come to reach your fullest potential in G-d. I pray He helps you to overcome barriers that have hindered you. I pray that you are ushered into a richer and deeper knowledge of the only true, very much alive and Eternal King - the G-d of Abraham, Isaac and Jacob.

You may find some of the contents of this book up for debate. You might agree with some points and you might vehemently disagree with other points. My words may fall short, however the Words of G-d are Truth. God's Words are alive, active and perfect.

The writer of the Book of Hebrews spoke about the power of the word of God. His word is "sharper than any two-edged sword, piercing even to the dividing asunder of soul and spirit, and of the joints and marrow, and is a discerner of the thoughts and intents of the heart." (Hebrews 4:12)

Rabbinic tradition also gives weight to the validity of Torah, and the sacredness of the Words of God.

Whether you agree or disagree as you read through this book, I implore you to read it through to the very end, and to just be open, throughout, as you contemplate its contents. Take any lingering questions directly to Adonai. He will definitely answer as you seek Him.

AN INTRODUCTION TO THE TEHILLIM (PSALMS)

The Hebrew word for "Psalms" is "Tehillim" which means "songs of praise". The Psalms contain many beautiful prayers, hymns and also prophetic words. Many Jewish people have used the Psalms in liturgy and prayer. Many also read a portion from Tehillim daily, along with their daily readings from Torah (first five books of the Bible) and Talmud (the collection of studies and commentaries on the Torah). We are going to begin the journey by looking specifically at Psalm 118 in this study.

Psalm 118 is part of a group of Psalms known as "The Hallel". The word "Hallel" is Hebrew for "Praise". The "Hallel" consists of Psalms 113-118. These Psalms are recited at specific times in the synagogue, during certain Jewish Holy days, expressing thanks and praise for God and God's redemption.

Various Psalms have proven to have portions that are prophetic. Jewish commentaries and rabbis of old have recognized that the prophecies and the references found in the Biblical texts, point to a coming Messiah.

It is indeed exciting to read and unfold the meaning of the various Biblical texts, to explore the prophecies, and to gain wisdom from the Words of our Creator. The Words of God are for life, well-being, and nourishment to the soul. I pray, that as you explore and contemplate, you are nourished through this revealing study of God's Word.

Let's look now specifically at Psalm 118.

1

LIFE THROUGH MERCY

"*O give thanks unto the LORD; for he is good: because his mercy endureth for ever. Let Israel now say, that his mercy endureth for ever. Let the house of Aaron now say, that his mercy endureth for ever. Let them now that fear the LORD say, that his mercy endureth for ever.*"
(Psalm 118:1-4)

The Psalmist here begins by focusing first on God. Certainly, our focus too should be first and foremost on Him. Torah also focuses first on God. The first few words in Bereshit (Hebrew word for

15

the first book of the Bible, Genesis) show, right from the start, the focus of the Holy Scriptures. Genesis begins with the words, "In the beginning **God...**"

Before man existed, before the earth was created, before the heavens were parted, was and is the eternal God. It is to Him, the Creator of all the

> *OUR FOCUS, FIRST AND FOREMOST, SHOULD BE ON GOD.*

universe, that we are to give all adoration, praise and thanks.

In order for us to fully give God praise, we need to recognize Who He is. God is our Hope, our Life, our Maker, our Creator. He is God. He is the answer to our deepest needs. He is our Victory, and our Strength.

God is our Redeemer Who gives Truth, Wisdom, and new beginnings.

Are you ready for a new beginning in your life? Sometimes for us to embrace the new, we have to say goodbye to what is old. Old thoughts, old ways of thinking, may be hindering your growth in God and your commitment to Him. Sometimes it is in the endings of some things in our lives that the most beautiful of new beginnings can come about. Sometimes it is only in the ending of old ways, old habits, old traditions, that new breakthroughs can come. Endings can be good. Endings can be enriching. Endings can play a vital role in clearing the path ahead to make way for that which is the very best path for your life.

Think about where you are in life right now. Can you identify things in your life right now that may be hindering you, weighing you down, taking from you, or keeping you from being all that you are meant to be? You might be bogged down because of the crowd you hang out with, or because of a particular relationship, or unwise business connections. Is there something keeping you from reaching your potential? Is there anything in your life right now that you know isn't the very best for you, isn't what is good and right? That thing could really be robbing from your life, and stealing from your life's potential.

It could be that now is <u>your</u> time for change. A change for the better has perhaps been long overdue. This may be your time to refocus on what really matters. What really matters, and what is above all things is God. More important than any business venture, partnership

> **THIS MAY BE YOUR TIME TO REFOCUS ON WHAT REALLY MATTERS. ABOVE ALL THINGS IS <u>GOD</u>.**

or material possession is God. He created you, and He has the purpose for your life, which you can discover, as you keep Him first.

Keeping 1st Things First

Solomon, most likely the writer of the book of Ecclesiastes, after a long discussion about the weights and burdens of life, comes to a very wise conclusion, as he calls it, **"the conclusion to the whole matter"**. Solomon had all the wealth the world could offer. In addition, G-d had given

Solomon all the wisdom to make the best business and best management decisions. Solomon had access, authority, and power to have all that his eyes desired. Yet with all his prosperity, he comes to a humbling conclusion. After pondering where his life had taken him, and after considering all the works of his hands, all that his labor had brought him, he realized there was something in life that was much more important.

With all of Solomon's wisdom and understanding, with all of his understanding of wonders, sciences, and insight into the why's of life, with all of his in-

> *"FEAR GOD AND KEEP HIS COMMANDMENTS..."*

depth analyzing of the true meaning and value of existence, he is led, in the end, to state this: "Now all has been heard, here is the conclusion of the matter: **Fear God, and keep his commandments, for this is the duty of all mankind.**" (Eccl 12:11)

Solomon who possessed all that the world could

offer, came to see the <u>futility</u> of all that the world could offer. The focus of his eyes moved from worldly "things" and worldly purpose to something deeper and more permanent: What was his purpose in the world? Why was he put on this earth? Solomon's conclusion was God-centered.

Now consider this serious question. Do you know <u>your</u> purpose in the world? Why were you put here on this earth, in this particular time of history, in your particular location, wherever it may be? Short and sweet: WHY ARE YOU HERE?

The wisest man on all the earth reasoned and rightly concluded that the only way to understand such things is to consider <u>God's</u> ways, to understand and to know God more fully, and as a result, in reverence, awe and wonder of God, to worship Him.

Is the focus of your life God-centered? The Creator of all the earth may be calling you this very day to take a deeper

> *YOUR LIFE AND TRUE LIFE-PURPOSE IS FOUND IN GOD.*

look, and to realize that your life and true life purpose is found in Him.

In Biblical times, the sounding of the shofar was used to make a proclamation. It was used as a battle cry, to usher in something new, to herald a victorious event. It was used as a warning, and as an alarm.

This book has a purpose - to make a proclamation, to alert, to announce, to declare to you personally what God's Word says. God's Truth can usher you into something richer and deeper. The Truth of God's Word can bring you to endings and bring you to new beginnings, so that you may be open to come to the same conclusion that Solomon did - the vital realization, the conclusion of the whole matter - to obey God, to fear Him.

To fear God means that you look to Him with utmost respect. It means that you stand in awe of Him. This will happen when you truly seek Him with your heart. When you seek Him, you can begin to see His power, His attributes and His sovereignty over all things. The beginning of your journey to find success, well-being, peace and life-purpose starts when you open your heart and make the decision to diligently seek Him Who created you, as Solomon sought and found.

Who is God to you? Who is He that holds your next breath in His hands? Who is He Who loves you enough to die for you? Who is He and why do you need to know Him?

Torah states it like this: "Who is like unto thee, O LORD, among the gods? who is like thee, glorious in holiness, fearful in praises, doing wonders?" Shemot (Exodus) 15:11

In Hebrew, it's "Micha mocha ba'elim, Adonai". Who is like unto Thee, Hashem. Among all the "gods" that the world claims, there is no other god. No one can do the acts and wonders in creation that Adonai can do. When we truly come to realize this, then humility, praise, adoration, and worship will rightly follow.

When you understand Who God is, as Torah teaches, then you will begin to see Who God is in your individual life - Who He is for YOU! You will see how the beloved of your soul

> *THE BELOVED OF YOUR SOUL HAS BEEN CALLING YOU.*

has been calling you, and drawing you to Himself even before the time He formed you in the womb. **His purpose and plan for you is that you seek Him, learn of Him, grow in Him, and embrace Him fully.**

This may be your time to leave behind what hinders you, to move out from where you've been entangled, to do the right thing. Like Solomon, you can ask the Living G-d all of your "why" questions. Ask God whatever it is that you want to understand more deeply. Seek Him, learn of Him, get to know Him better. Move the focus of your eyes away from what the world provides as solutions. Focus instead on Who your Creator is. Focus on what His Word says. That's where you'll find the answers. Allow God to reveal all that He has to offer you, because of His great love for you!

With the proper focus, keeping first things first, all the other priorities and details of life, the needs, goals, and desires, will be given their proper place, and will be taken care of by God. For it is G-d Himself Who always provides in His measure, in His way. It is God Who knows what is best for your life. God will provide.

Today, set aside the weights of the heart, and look to Him. Only G-d can bring about the needed changes on your behalf, if you seek Him diligently from your heart. Are you willing to seek Him? What is hindering you from taking these vital steps towards Him? Is your heart burdened right now? Allow Him to lift those heavy burdens and weights from your life. He can set you free. He is more than capable. He is G-d.

Start now with a simple prayer asking Him to give you proper focus, to clarify your vision, to show Himself strong to you, to reveal Himself to you in a more personal way from this day forward. Allow God to open your heart, and to give you your life's vision and purpose.

This journey through Psalm 118 is a first step to seeing your life purpose, giving you a glimpse into Who God is, and His plan for you, His plan for His chosen people, and His plan for the generations, through the ages.

Be Thankful for His Goodness

Today, consider all the things for which you can be thankful. We should say as the Psalmist said in verse one: "O give thanks unto the Lord".

We probably have many things for which we can give thanks, but the Psalmist here focuses on God's goodness and mercy. The Hebrew word used here for "good" is "towb" (tobe) meaning good, pleasant, beautiful. It is the same word used in Genesis when it says G-d created the heavens and the earth and saw that it was "good". God who created all things is Himself good, pure, righteous, holy. He is righteous in <u>all</u> His ways. His ways are perfect, His ways are always good.

It may be hard to fathom, but the same good and righteous God who created all the earth, Who spun the worlds into existence, Who at His word said "Let there be light" and there was, is the same God who created you.

Think about that!

God who created the intricacies of all the stars and the heavens, created you! Psalm 139 puts it beautifully, telling us that God created your inmost being. God says that He knit you together in your mother's womb. Scriptures say that even before He formed you, He knew you. "Thine eyes did see my substance, yet being unperfect; and in thy book all my members were written, which in continuance were fashioned, when as yet there was none of them. How precious also are thy thoughts unto me, O

> "...IN THY BOOK ALL MY MEMBERS WERE WRITTEN, WHICH IN CONTINUANCE WERE FASHIONED, WHEN AS YET THERE WAS NONE OF THEM..."

God! how great is the sum of them!" (Psalm 139:16-17)

God created you personally in His exact way, perfectly prescribed, and set specifically at this moment in all history, exactly as He planned. He made you and He knows everything about you. Nothing is hidden from Him. He knows when you get up, and when you sit down. He knows when you are happy, and He knows when you feel like you are bearing the weight of the world.

God made you precisely. He knows your ups and downs, your highs and lows. He knows even the very number of hairs on your head. He knows and created your specific detailed DNA structure. He knows when you took your first breath, and He knows the exact second that you will take your last breath.

God created you intricately and specifically so that you may know Who He is. He is a personal Creator. He is your personal Creator! He is not an impersonal force. He is not an uncaring energy. He is a living and personal God. He created you to have a personal relationship with Him. He Who is perfect, Whose ways are good, delights to show you Who He is, but you must look.

God will show you Who He is and who you really are. He will show you His goodness. He will show Himself true, alive, and strong in your life as you look to Him. We all can thank God for how good, wonderful and magnificent He is.

In the Light of a Holy God

Psalm 118 speaks of God's goodness. Only God is truly good. Only God is perfect in all His ways. This attribute of God - His goodness - shows not only who He is, but also sheds light on who we are. Only God is pure, righteous, and without fault. There is no darkness and no sin in Him. Only He is good and totally pure and perfectly Holy in every way.

Where do we stand in the light of a good and Holy God? Are we flawless and perfect in our ways? No, none of us are perfectly pure. Every one of us falls short, very far short, of perfection. All our righteousness, as the prophet Isaiah declares, is as filthy rags (Is 64:6). We are unclean compared to a Holy and perfect God. Even the best of all our own works, the most generous of all acts of charity, even with our most diligent observance of all decrees, we still fall very far short of God's perfect perfection.

We can never do enough or be enough on our own, to meet the standards and perfection of our most Holy God.

So, how can we, imperfect since the fall of Adam, have a deep intimate relationship with God Who is totally perfect and pure? Here is where the mystery of God's love is revealed. Enter grace. Enter mercy. Enter atonement. Enter God's great and perfect love - for you!

The perfect God, the Creator of all the earth, through His grace and mercy, makes a way for us to draw close to Him. There's a huge gap between our unholiness and God's holiness. But God bridges the gap. God has made the way. HaShem (Adonai, God) Himself, because of His deep love for His own, has bridged the gap. He has made a way, so that even with our faults, spots, blemishes, weaknesses and imperfections, we can draw close to Him Who is perfect and without sin. We can never do this on our own. It is not by anything we can accomplish in our own strength. It is not through our own ingenuity or our own power, but relationship with the Almighty God comes only through God's very special provision and plan, through His grace and His mercy.

The Psalmist knows of grace, and can say boldly "His mercies endure forever". Because of God's goodness and His mercies toward us, we can have a relationship with our Creator. Because of His grace and provision, we can stand before our Holy King. When we focus on His attributes, His way of atonement, His goodness, grace and mercy, we can then have a relationship with Him, and offer our praises to our good and merciful Creator.

We can say "His mercies endure forever". Not only can we say it, but the Psalmist goes on in verse 2 to say: Let all Israel say it too!

The Israel Blessing Connection:

The Importance of Israel

Why Israel? Let's take a deeper look at God's plan through the ages for His beloved Israel.

The name "Israel" is from Hebrew, meaning "God contended". It involves wrestling and triumph. It involves struggle, but also victory. It was given as a name for Jacob who, as told in Genesis 32, wrestled with an angel, struggled and fought to obtain a blessing from God. Jacob's life, though, was often marked by failures and weakness. Jacob's life was imperfect, as ours is imperfect. Yet God was good and merciful to Jacob. God showed mercy to Jacob when He confronted Jacob. It was in Jacob's struggle, as he wrestled and fought, that Jacob realized his own weakness and saw God's strength. Read the account in Genesis 32:24-30.

God saw Jacob's struggles and weaknesses, and in His grace, chose to bless Jacob's life and fulfill His promises to Jacob. Jacob was chosen of God, even though Jacob had weaknesses and sin. Yet God had grace.

Jacob was given the new name of "Israel", and as God had promised Abraham, a nation was born through his lineage. Through Jacob was born twelve sons, the twelve tribes of Israel.

This nation is the nation God has chosen, as priests, to be set apart to declare His praises, and to keep His ways. His people were to adhere to His laws, to follow diligently, and to teach His good ways to their children, and to their children's children.

Like Jacob, the people and nation of Israel have also struggled tremendously, and even wrestled, to obtain God's blessing. It was however, God's goodness and mercy that prevailed for Jacob, and likewise, always *will* prevail for His chosen people.

By His grace, God has continued to bless His chosen people and continued to prosper the land of Israel. God's commitment is to keep His promises for Israel. God brings life out of darkness. God raised Israel up from desolation to become a land of prosperity. Though we may not fully understand it, God will continue to work

> *GOD'S PROMISES FOR THE NATION OF ISRAEL ARE CLEARLY DECLARED THROUGHOUT ALL THE BIBLE.*

out all of the world's details, all the current world situations, and all the world's strife, so that all of His good promises for Israel and His people are fulfilled.

God's promises for the nation of Israel are clearly declared throughout all the Bible. God has not abandoned, or forgotten His people – even when His people have walked away from Him.

Scriptures record the times that God's beloved and chosen Jewish people have often drifted away from God, and were led astray by pagan ways. Yet, because of God's great love and mercy, God has been faithful to keep His covenant of love to His people through all generations. From Biblical times, until the end of this age, God's mercies for Israel endure forever.

The promises for Israel stand strong. The promises have not been abrogated, but the covenant holds firm. God has promised to bless Israel, to keep Israel, save Israel, restore Israel, and to give Israel the expected and glorious inheritance - ultimately bringing His peace. No act of man or cleverly woven human strategy can change that.

Torah says that all nations shall be blessed through His people. God said to Abraham, "... And in thy seed shall all the nations of the earth be blessed..." (Genesis 22:18) Not only are His people blessed, but God promises

> *"AND I WILL BLESS THEM THAT BLESS THEE..."*

blessings also to those who bless Israel. He says, **"And I will make of thee a great nation, and I will** bless thee, and make thy name great; and thou shalt be a blessing: And I will bless them that bless thee, and curse him that curseth thee: and in thee shall all families of the earth be blessed." (Genesis 12:2-3)

Just by blessing His people, you will be blessed! Isn't this something for which we can thank God! As the Psalmist says in verse one, "O give thanks unto the LORD; for he is good: because his mercy endureth forever."

Many are the promises and provisions and blessings of God to all those who know Him. God is good and His mercies endure forever.

It is indeed something we can be glad about! So, let all Israel say it! Let all those who lovingly join hands with Israel to serve the God of Abraham, Isaac and Jacob say it! May all who look to see God's good promises fulfilled for His people, receive the blessing, and let all of us rejoice and give thanks!

May all Israel see, take hold of, and thank God

for His mercies. **May all Israel praise God for His goodness.** *"Let Israel now say, that his mercy endureth for ever."* (Psalm 118:2)

The High Priest's Atonement

Psalm 118 verse 3 goes on to say: *"Let the house of Aaron now say, that his mercy endureth for ever."* Those given the high calling and honor of being in the house of Aaron can say it.

And who is in the **house of Aaron?**

In the Torah, Aaron, the brother of Moshe (Moses), great-grandson of Levi, was set apart by God to carry out the priestly duties of the temple. He was consecrated and anointed of God to

> *GOD SAID TO MOSES, "FOR THE LIFE OF THE FLESH IS IN THE BLOOD: AND I HAVE GIVEN IT TO YOU UPON THE ALTAR..."*

preserve and protect the sanctuary, to carry out the sacrificial offerings on behalf of the people so that, through the sacrifice by the High Priest, there could be atonement for their sins. Aaron, in obedience to the call of God, fulfilled his priestly duties in offering the sacrifice. God then accepted the sacrificial offering and forgave the transgressions of his people. In the temple, God then blessed the people with His presence and the glory of the Lord filled the house. That was God's plan of sacrifice and atonement which was set up in Torah.

The priestly duties and the offerings of sacrifice continued for generations. The sacrificial system was set up by God as the way to meet His requirement for sinless perfection. For who can stand before a Holy God! Unrighteousness cannot abide with a Righteous God. How can we have the relationship that God desires us to have with Him, if we ourselves are not perfectly righteous? In Leviticus 17:11, God gives the answer to

> *A SACRIFICE AND ATONEMENT HAD TO BE MADE IN ORDER FOR MAN, IN HIS FALLEN STATE, TO HAVE PEACE AND PRESENCE WITH HIS RIGHTEOUS CREATOR.*

Moshe (Moses) "For the life of the flesh is in the blood: and I have given it to you upon the altar to make an atonement for your souls: **for it is the blood that maketh an atonement** for the soul."

God, because of His love for His people, made a way for unrighteousness and sin to be dealt with, through atonement. **A sacrifice and atonement had to be made in order for man, in his fallen state, to have peace and presence with his righteous Creator.** The way God made for us to enjoy the fullness of God's blessing, and to have a relationship with Him is through sacrifice and atonement.

The sacrificial system was set up so that generations could enjoy the sweet fellowship and pure relationship with Him Who is holy.

Have things changed since the days of animal sacrifice? Man has not changed over the years. Man's sin nature is evidently still in existence, and has been since the time of Adam. Adam chose to sin rather than to obey God's one simple command to not eat of one particular tree in the Garden of Eden.

Adam and Eve chose to eat of the one tree that God had forbidden them. They chose to go their own way, rather than God's way. Similarly, we often choose to not obey God, choosing rather to do things our way, to compromise, to resist Him.

Man's imperfection still shows itself since Adam. Our sin shows itself through our pride, through harmful desires, anger, lusts, even through one straying thought. We easily find ourselves disobeying God's plan. Our natural tendency is to stray from God. Anything short of perfection and total purity separates us from our Holy Creator. So then, if we all still have our sin nature, how can we, today, be restored to perfect fellowship with a perfectly Holy God?

God doesn't leave us without answers. He gives us a prescribed way to deal with sin. **The way God ordained to cover sin was through atonement, through a sacrifice, through the** shedding of the blood of a perfect lamb.

We know God is just and requires holiness.

God is also a loving God, Who shows us His mercy and great love for us by making a way of atonement - through a sacrifice. We know that.

THE WAY GOD ORDAINED TO COVER SIN WAS THROUGH ATONEMENT, THROUGH A SACRIFICE, THROUGH THE SHEDDING OF THE BLOOD OF A PERFECT LAMB.

A spotless and innocent lamb bore the punishment of sin. Through the death of the lamb, and shedding of the lamb's own blood, the way of atonement was made. God, Who is just and righteous, accepted the sacrifice, and forgave man's sin through the sacrifice.

The priestly tribe of Aaron would bring the sacrifice to the altar as atonement for the sins of the people. **The sacrifice became the substitute, to die in the place of the man whose sins**

convicted him in the presence of the perfect, just and holy Judge. The perfect holiness of God, along with His attribute of perfect love, combined to make the perfect way of atonement, so that we would not be punished for our sins as we deserve.

Sin separates us from God, but the ATONEMENT allows us to be united as one with Him. Atonement is often said to bring us to the state of "at-one-ment" with God, so that sinful man can come before a sinless God, and receive the blessings of His presence again - to be, in a sense, one with Him.

> *THE SACRIFICE BECAME THE SUBSTITUTE, TO DIE IN THE PLACE OF THE MAN WHOSE SINS CONVICTED HIM...*

So, the house of Aaron, who has made atonement through sacrifice, can say that God's mercy endures forever. As the Psalmist says, we can say "His mercies never fail".

God is the same yesterday, today and forever. In His love, generations ago, He made the way through sacrifice of an innocent lamb to pay the price for man's sins, and to redeem His people. In His grace and love today, God has made a way through sacrifice to redeem us, to pay for our sins.

Not only did God make the way for a sacrifice to be given, but His love was and is so great for us, that He was willing to become that spotless, blameless, perfect sacrificial Lamb, Himself bearing all our sins upon Him, to once and for all make the necessary atonement for the sins of mankind, to all who would accept and believe. How great a love is that!! Think about it!

That is something to truly rejoice about!

2

THOUGH THERE BE OPPOSITION

"*I* called upon the LORD in distress: the LORD answered me, and set me in a large place. The LORD is on my side; I will not fear: what can man do unto me. The LORD taketh my part with them that help me: therefore shall I see my desire upon them that hate me." *(Psalm 118:5-7)*

Not only can we rejoice in the God's atoning work, but we can rejoice in His provision in times of

43

trouble, in times of stress and distress. There is a name that we can call on for help. It is the name of the Living G-d. Anytime of the day or night, He is there. Through any situation, we can call out to Him. God, Who is Sovereign and in control of every detail, hears.

The Psalmist declares here that the Lord is on his side. For those who seek the Lord, the Lord is on your side too. You don't have to fear. There is nothing that man can do to you that will take you away from God, Who is with you always.

God is your defense. He is Israel's defense. He is the Defender of the poor, the weak, the orphan, the widow, the downtrodden, the abused. The Psalms are filled with promises for those who look to Him in their time of trouble. "The LORD also will be a refuge for the oppressed, a refuge in times of trouble." (Psalm 9:9)

"LORD, thou hast heard the desire of the humble: thou wilt prepare their heart, thou wilt cause thine ear to hear: To judge the fatherless and the oppressed, that the man of the earth may no more oppress." (Psalm 10:17-18)

The Lord promises strength for the weak, and listens to the cries of the humble.

When trouble, fear, and terror come, we can call on the Lord. God, Who knows all and sees all, will come to our defense, as He has, time after time, come to defend His beloved Israel and has preserved and protected her throughout the generations.

God is on our side, and will never abandon us, and He will always do all that is best for us, to bring us back to Himself. He may, at times, chasten us as a loving father chastens the children he loves. Through whatever comes our way, God will always be with us to help, as we call out to Him.

Take a first step and call out to Him today. It doesn't have to be a long elaborate prayer, it can be a simple "Lord, I need help...". Just make it a call from your heart. At any hour of the day or night, you may call out, pour out your thoughts to Him, and look to Him to provide the answer. Tell him your struggles and fears. Bring to Him your anxieties, shortcomings, and weakness. **Be honest before Him and tell Him about the burdens you are carrying today.** He will take care of you, and the situation. He is able to not only help you, but God can control perfectly and adequately all the details involved. He will not only help you, but will also handle perfectly all the people involved in your situation. He is able to deal with any who oppress you, and God even has the ability to touch their lives too, drawing them to Him as well.

Call out to God today with your struggles, and you will see, as the Psalmist saw. Though there be opposition, you will say *"I called upon the LORD in my distress, and the LORD answered me."'*

3

RELYING ON WHO?!

"*I*t is better to trust in the LORD than to put confidence in man. It is better to trust in the LORD than to put confidence in princes." (Psalm 118:8-9)*

Stated simply, only God is God. There is only One Who called into existence all that is, at the sound of His Word. **God is the only One Who created things** which are seen out of things which

47

are not seen. It is this God to Whom we can run in our times of need. It is this God Who we can trust at <u>all</u> times. Man might offer a temporary fix or a little comfort, but only God can provide absolutely <u>everything</u> that we need.

Who are you putting your trust in today? Man is limited, God is unlimited. Man will always fall short of the highest expectations. Even princes and kings who have great resources available, won't always be there for you. All of man's resources can in no way match the endless resources that God has available for you. Who but God truly has your best interests at heart?! Who but God can cause all things to work out for your good?

When faced with a dilemma, though man can offer man's solution, only God has all power, to do <u>anything</u> on your behalf, in an instant of time. Nothing is too hard or difficult for God. Nothing is impossible for God.

The God Who made you, loves you, and cares about every detail that touches your life, will indeed come to your rescue, if you just ask Him.

Would you like to call on God for assistance to rescue you from a particular situation you're facing today? Ask Him today for help. God is able to rescue and deliver you. He can rescue from the addiction, from that habit. God can rescue you from any area of struggle. He is your refuge, your deliverer, and will do above and beyond what any man can do for you.

The Bible says, "Ask, and it shall be given you; seek, and ye shall find; knock, and it shall be opened unto you: For every one that asketh receiveth; and he that seeketh findeth; and to him that knocketh it shall be opened. For what man is there of you, whom if his son ask bread, will he give him a stone? Or if he ask a fish, will he give him a serpent? If ye then, being evil, know how to give good gifts unto your children, how much more shall your Father which is in heaven give good things to them that ask him? Therefore all things whatsoever ye would that men should do to you, do ye even so to them: for this is the law and the prophets."

(Matthew, the Jewish disciple, 7:7-12)

God, Who alone is God, will do more than you ever could ask or hope for. You can always count on God. He will always give you what is best. He will give you all that you really need. Just ask Him.

4

AGAINST ALL ODDS

" *A*ll nations compassed me about: but in the name of the LORD will I destroy them. They compassed me about; yea, they compassed me about: but in the name of the LORD I will destroy them. They compassed me about like bees: they are quenched as the fire of thorns: for in the name of the LORD I will destroy them. Thou hast thrust sore at me that I might fall: but the LORD helped me. The LORD is my strength and song, and is become my salvation. " (Psalm 118:10-14)

51

Our attention is now brought to the nations who surround and oppress, yet the Psalmist here shows the victory gained when the oppressed look in faith to God. What people have known great trials and oppression from nations more than the people of Israel? Though nations have oppressed and though peoples have sought to obliterate Israel off the face of the

> *AGAINST ALL ODDS, GOD HAS PRESERVED HIS PEOPLE. THE NATION OF ISRAEL HAS GOD'S BLESSING.*

map, God's promise to preserve Israel remains and has proven true. Though there has been hatred of Jews through the ages, God's promise, His commitment and love for His chosen people prevails.

Against all odds, God has preserved and protected His people. The nation of Israel has God's blessing.

This infuriates the enemies of God.

Enemies of God, and enemies of God's chosen people, have sought for generations to oppress and destroy Israel. From Haman's plot to destroy the Jews (detailed in the book of Esther), to Hitler's plan in the Holocaust, to the terrorism and anti-Semitism we see today, there is nothing, and there is no one

> *ISRAEL IS THE APPLE OF GOD'S EYE. THROUGH ISRAEL, THE REDEEMER COMES, AND GOD'S PEOPLE ARE SAVED.*

who can stand against God. Though there be strife and conflict causing much pain and multiplied sorrows, there is nothing that will thwart God's plan and His preservation of the nation He's blessed and called. He will not disavow His covenant relationship with His people. God's promises stand for all eternity. Those who are fighting against God's people and God's plan are themselves fighting against God Himself. They will never win in their fight against God.

We need to pray for those who oppose God. There's truth about God that they are missing. If they search for it, they may find it. Pray God draws them, to open their hearts to His Love and His Truth. Pray for the peace of Jerusalem.

Israel is the apple of God's eye. Through Israel, the Redeemer comes, and His people are saved.

Against all odds, a people who had been scattered in the world have been miraculously preserved. It is by God's grace.

Prophetic Words Concerning Israel

After many years of being scattered, the Jewish people are now being brought back to once again serve and worship the One True and Living God in their own nation.

All that was spoken by God in the Holy Scriptures has and will be fulfilled. Let's take a look at some of the Scriptures and what the Jewish prophets had to say about the nation of Israel.

The prophet Isaiah describes a time of travail, birth and preservation. "Before she travailed, she brought forth; before her pain came, she was delivered of a man child. Who hath heard such a thing? who hath seen such things? Shall the earth be made to bring forth in one day? or shall a nation be born at once? for as soon as Zion travailed, she brought forth her children. Shall I bring to the birth, and not cause to bring forth? saith the LORD: shall I cause to bring forth, and shut the womb? saith thy God."

(Isaiah 66:7-9)

After many trials, wars, hardships and threatened annihilations, a nation in 1948 was indeed brought forth in a day - just as was prophesied by the Jewish prophet. Israel became a nation.

The prophet Jeremiah foretold of a regathering "Therefore, behold, the days come, saith the LORD, that it shall no more be said, The LORD liveth, that brought up the children of Israel out of the land of Egypt; But, The LORD liveth, that brought up the children of Israel from the land of the north, and from all the lands whither he had driven them: and I will bring them again into their land that I gave unto their fathers." (Jeremiah 16:14-15)

"And I will be found of you, saith the LORD: and I will turn away your captivity, and I will gather you from all the nations, and from all the places whither I have driven you, saith the LORD; and I will bring you again into the place whence i caused you to be carried away **captive.**" (Jeremiah 29:14)

Ezekiel also prophesied of Israel's future. "I will accept you with your sweet savour, when I bring you out from the people, and

> *"I SHALL BRING YOU INTO THE LAND OF ISRAEL..."*

gather you out of the countries wherein ye have been scattered; and I will be sanctified in you before the heathen. **And ye shall know that I am the LORD, when I shall bring you into the land of Israel, into the country for the which I lifted up mine hand to give it to your fathers.**" (You can read this in Ezekiel 20:41-42)

Ezekiel also prophesied of a time that God Himself would sovereignly and miraculously bring back to life what was considered dead and impossible - when it seemed like all was hopeless.

Ezekiel was taken to a valley full of dry and disconnected bones. He said of the bones "indeed they were very dry" Yet God asked Ezekiel, "Can

> *"...BEHOLD, I WILL CAUSE BREATH TO ENTER INTO YOU, AND YE SHALL LIVE..."*

these bones live?" (Ezekiel 37:3) God told Ezekiel to prophesy to the bones saying "Again he said unto me, Prophesy upon these bones, and say unto them, O ye dry bones, hear the word of the LORD. Thus saith the Lord GOD unto **these bones; Behold, I will cause breath to enter into you, and ye shall live: And I will lay sinews upon you, and will bring up flesh upon you, and cover you with skin, and put breath in you, and ye shall live; and ye shall know that I am the LORD.**" (Ezekiel 37:4-6)

And it was so. God brought the dry bones together, and added sinews and flesh, and gave breath for the dry bones to be renewed and brought back to life - to live again. And as it said, "and the breath came into them, and they lived, and stood up upon their feet, an exceeding great army."

(Ezekiel 37:10b)

And so that there's no doubt regarding how this is being interpreted, God further specifically explains these words to Ezekiel and explains it for all of us now (in verses 11-14): "..these bones are the whole house of Israel: behold, they say, Our bones are dried, and our hope is lost: we are cut off for our parts.

"AND YE SHALL KNOW THAT I AM THE LORD, WHEN I HAVE OPENED YOUR GRAVES, AND SHALL PUT MY SPIRIT IN YOU, AND YE SHALL LIVE, AND I SHALL PLACE YOU IN YOUR OWN LAND..."

Therefore prophesy and say unto them, Thus saith the Lord GOD; Behold, O my people, I will open your graves, and cause you to come up out of your graves, and bring you into the land of Israel."

"And ye shall know that I am the LORD, when I have opened your graves, O my people, and brought you up out of your graves, And shall put my spirit in you, and ye shall live, and I shall place

> *"I SHALL PLACE YOU IN YOUR OWN LAND: THEN SHALL YE KNOW THAT I THE LORD HAVE SPOKEN IT, AND PERFORMED IT, SAITH THE LORD."*

you in your own land: then shall ye know that I the LORD have spoken it, and performed it, saith the LORD." (Ezekiel 37:11-14)

All things are possible with God. All that God has promised and spoken was, and is, being fulfilled.

"Since thou wast precious in my sight, thou hast been honourable, and I have loved thee: therefore will I give men for thee, and people for thy life. Fear not: for I am with thee: **I will bring thy seed from the east, and gather thee from the west; I will say** to the north, Give up; and to the south, Keep not back: bring my sons from far, and my daughters from the ends of the earth; Even every one that is called by my name: for I have created him for my glory, I have formed him; yea, I have made him."

(Isaiah 43: 4-7)

No matter the trials, the swarming bees, and nations surrounding Israel, no matter the hatred against God and His people, the Lord will, in faithfulness, fulfill all His good promises to help and protect Israel.

God protects His beloved. All who love God and all who love Israel, can rejoice in His blessings.

We can rejoice in God's protection, preservation, and provision for eternal life. We can rejoice when God has made our own dry places to thrive again.

We can rejoice in how God has spared our lives, how He's given us life, how He's protected us in times when it seemed impossible.

We can rejoice in God's saving grace, in His salvation, through whatever trials we face.

All who follow Him, can join together and say indeed, as in Psalm 118 verse 12, "they compassed me about like bees" but "the Lord is my strength and song, and is become my salvation".

5

GOD GIVES US REASON TO REJOICE

"The voice of rejoicing and salvation is in the tabernacles of the righteous: the right hand of the LORD doeth valiantly. The right hand of the LORD is exalted: the right hand of the LORD doeth valiantly." (Psalm 118:15-16)

The people of God are characterized by rejoicing. In the tabernacles of God's people there can be heard the voices of

> **THOSE WHO GOD REDEEMS ARE CHARACTERIZED BY REJOICING AND PRAISE.**

rejoicing and salvation. The reason for such joy is God Himself. God alone redeems and saves. He brings victory and does valiantly on behalf of those who trust in Him. God alone is the one to be praised and glorified. He brings us out of bondage and gives us cause to rejoice, to praise and honor Him with our voices.

Victory is in God, through His right hand, and by His valiant works. Those who know this personally will express it. In the sanctuary we can hear the voices of praise and joy.

The Choice of Voices

There are many voices to be heard in the world, but in His sanctuary, there are voices of rejoicing.

Take time now to compare and contrast the various voices that can be heard these days. The voice of peace vs. the voice of distress. The voice of love vs. the voice of dissention and division. The voice of worry vs. the voice of hope.

The world is full of troubles and it's easy to get caught up in the current events, the news voices of the day, the unrest, the controversies and strife, the fears and worries.

With all the distractions of life, can you truly take time to hear <u>God's</u> voice and to rejoice in <u>God</u>? Are you spending time looking into God's Word, learning of Him, taking hold of His promises? Or is the world pulling you away from your Creator? How much time do we spend listening to the world's voices, instead of God's truth?

How many hours a day do you spend chewing on, and eating up all the negative? It can become all-consuming, not only time-consuming, but also physically consuming, stealing you of peace and well-being. The world can bring no lasting peace, no inner joy, and no cause for rejoicing. The world and the world's solutions cannot bring about the praise spoken of by the Psalmist.

Is your voice able to sing the praises of God?

Your speech is a revealer of what you value. Your speech shines an exposing light on the contents

> YOUR SPEECH IS A REVEALER OF YOUR HEART AND YOUR PRIORITIES.

of your heart, and on your priorities in life.

Examine your own words. Compare and contrast. What is your speech, your voice, revealing about your heart and your priorities? Do you spend time building others up, speaking well of others, and seeing the best in others, or do you find yourself often tearing others down, chiseling at their reputation, destroying their character? **Slander is a form of murder. It's murdering someone else's character. Don't engage in it. It will destroy you, as you seek to destroy another.** We all are prone because of pride and our sin nature to make others look bad so we can come out looking great. It's easy to fall into. However, we need to **choose a higher road** - to bring life and healing to yourself and others.

The Higher Road of Love

Only in God can we take the higher road to not only *see* the best in others, but to also *believe* the best about them, and help them to be their best. Only God's love can propel us to love others the way we should.

Love invests in others, and takes action to encourage others to be their best. Love doesn't gossip or murder another's

> *ONLY IN GOD CAN WE TAKE THE HIGHER ROAD... OF LOVE.*

character with harsh and slanderous words. Love doesn't judge, but trusts God who judges righteously. Love speaks the truth with the intention of helping and building up others to be their best. It's a sacrifice. It's hard to do at times, but it's the higher way. It's a way to bring blessing to your own life.

How much love do you have today? How much love do you show to others, by your words and actions?

Love bears all things, hopes all things, and believes the best about others, and seeks for their good, and acts on the behalf of others, for their good. God's love does this.

In this age of "selfies" and emphasis on self-importance, self-image, and self-love, <u>true</u> love actually shows itself not by putting *self* first, but by putting God first, and then shows itself through actions intended for the good of others.

Love is not blind to seeing weakness (we all have weaknesses), but love proves itself in how it responds to another's weakness. Are you a builder of character, or are you a destroyer of the character of another? Do you help to strengthen someone else's

> *SEEK TO LOSE YOURSELF IN LOVE...*

weakness, or do you try to expose it, for your own benefit? True love seeks the best and always takes the higher road. If you veer off the road now and again, get right back on the good path, and **seek to lose yourself in love.**

Is your voice a voice of love towards God and to others in your own life?

God's Glory in the Sanctuary

Now, let's compare and contrast again. This time, as it relates to what you hear in the sanctuary. What are you hearing in your place of worship? Compare and contrast. Is it a place where the presence of God is? Or is it a place where statues, rituals or entertainment has taken the place that God should hold?

What voices are you hearing at your place of worship? In your sanctuary are you hearing the voice of the latest fads, political issues or social events, or are you hearing, as the Psalmist highlights in verse 15, the "voice of rejoicing", and the words of salvation?

A true place of worship is a place that truly worships. The presence of God is there, the Scriptures are cherished and read, and God's words from His Holy Scriptures are spoken.

> *A TRUE PLACE OF WORSHIP IS A PLACE WHERE THE LOVE OF GOD DWELLS.*

There the voice of rejoicing can be heard.

The voice of rejoicing flows from the heart of those who love God. God is love. **Remember we love because He first loved us. God is the source. We can't really love without His love first.**

A true place of worship is a place where the love of God dwells.

Do you rejoice in your sanctuary? Is it the desire of your heart to become a true worshiper of God? Pray about this now. If you're not there yet, pray that God will open your heart so that you can rejoice as you worship, so that you can say from your heart, as is written in Psalm 63: "O God, thou art my God; early will I seek thee: my soul thirsteth for thee, my flesh longeth for thee in a dry and thirsty land, where no water is; **To see thy power and thy glory, so as I have seen thee in the sanctuary. Because thy lovingkindness is better than life, my lips shall praise thee.** Thus will I bless thee while I live: I will lift up my hands in thy name. My soul shall be satisfied as with marrow and fatness; and my mouth shall praise thee with joyful lips." (Psalm 63-1-5)

You may be at a point in your life where you have to make some choices that will change your life's direction dramatically. As you ponder, as you compare and contrast these important areas of your life, it is my heartfelt prayer that you commit to taking the higher road of love, and in love with your loving Saviour.

Allow God's love to fill your voice with rejoicing. Allow the voice of a loving Savior, the voice of God through His written Word, to fill your heart, and fill your time. Allow His love to show forth in your actions. Allow His Hands to touch, heal and strengthen each area of need in your life today. Allow God to lead you to a place of true worship and praise, where His love abides. Then God will give you the reason to really rejoice in Him!

6

YOUR PURPOSE

"*I* shall not die, but live, and declare the works of the LORD." (Psalm 118:17)

There's something about seeing death, being near death, facing your own illness, or even the quiet moments when sitting shiva (the time of mourning) or attending the funeral of a loved one, that causes one, even if ever so briefly, to **take a pause in life**. When we witness suffering, or experience suffering ourselves, we take a pause.

73

During these pauses, there are often times of reflection about life, and about the brevity of life. For a moment, we pause from the normal hustle and bustle.

> *THERE'S SOMETHING ABOUT SEEING DEATH THAT CAUSES US TO TAKE A PAUSE IN LIFE...*

When we have these pauses, we reflect, we grieve, we mourn, we maybe have our momentary "wake-up call", and for a few moments we may ponder what is most important in life.

Yet, too often and too quickly we forget, as the tidal wave of our normal routine sweeps us right back again into the normal routine. Too soon we slip back into dealing with the normal routine again, and the hustle and bustle again, again focusing on the lesser important.... until the next pause that God so carefully and lovingly orchestrates for our life.

Throughout the Ketuvim writings of Psalms and in the book of Habakkuk, there's a Hebrew word used that we too quickly gloss over. It's the word "selah". It seems to be placed here and there, what we may initially view as quite randomly. We often find it in between two sentences or thoughts. As we read the Scriptures we pass over this small word, to get to the next thought in the text. However, God in His inspired Word has placed the "selah" there for a reason. So, let's take a deeper look.

In Hebrew the meaning of the word "selah" is multi-faceted, like a rare and beautiful gem. It can carry with it various meanings, depending on how one is viewing it. When holding a gemstone up to the light, it can sparkle and glimmer as it is turned and viewed from various angles. In the same way, we can look deeper into the "selah's" of the text, and of life. By looking deeper, we can see great beauty and richness, if only we take the time to look, learn, and give heed to God's instruction.

So what does the word "selah" mean? There could be various dimensions and definitions. It may mean to stop, pause, and think further about. One aspect of the word suggested by the text, may mean to weigh the thought, as one would do when using a balance for weights and measures, also implying value. Another definition may be related to music, appropriately found in the Psalms, like a musical pause, or to lift up, exalt or praise.

When the "selah" is placed in the text, the idea behind it is that **it's time to take a pause, to stop, to reflect** on what you've just read. It's a time to look at a different facet of its meaning. It's a time we can dig deeper to contemplate. It's a time not to overlook a hidden beautiful aspect of the text that we've just read. It's a time not to gloss over, but to suspend the normal flow, and instead weigh, value, and look further. It's a time to ask God to give insight and personal application of the text to our lives.

The Selahs of Psalm 46

Although there are over 70 occurrences of the word "selah" in the book of Psalms, I will select one

Psalm containing several "Selah's" to show how to use this 'principle of pause', as a gem, to be a blessing for your life - to cast its ray of hope to shine life to your heart.

Psalm 46:

"God is our refuge and strength, a very present help in trouble. Therefore will not we fear, though the earth be removed, and though the mountains be carried into the midst of the sea; Though the waters thereof roar and be troubled, though the mountains shake with the swelling thereof. **SELAH.**"

(Psalm 46:1-3)

(Pause now, reflect, what is this saying. What did you just read, and what does it mean?)

"There is a river, the streams whereof shall make glad the city of God, the holy place of the tabernacles of the most High. God is in the midst of her; she shall not be moved: God shall help her, and that right early. The heathen raged, the kingdoms were moved: he uttered his voice, the earth melted.

The LORD of hosts is with us; the God of Jacob is our refuge. **SELAH**". (Psalm 46:4-7)

(Stop now, weigh the thought, dig deeper. What is God saying here about Israel?)

"Come, behold the works of the LORD, what desolations he hath made in the earth. He maketh wars to cease unto the end of the earth; he breaketh the bow, and cutteth the spear in sunder; he burneth the chariot in the fire. Be still, and know that I am God: I will be exalted among the heathen, I will be exalted in the earth. The LORD of hosts is with us; the God of Jacob is our refuge. **SELAH**" (Psalm 46:8-11)

(Pause, balance the words, contemplate the key points. Lift up, exalt, praise God Who gives understanding. What is God saying about His sovereignty over all things?)

By pausing, and reflecting more on these words, we can see the historic and the prophetic. The perfect accuracy of Biblical prophecy has been displayed in years past, and will be beautifully displayed in the years to come. Israel has seen God's sovereignty in His miraculous preserving of the land and His protection of His chosen people, despite wars being waged against her, and despite nations in uproar at Israel's rising. We can "SELAH", take time now to look at this in a deeper way.

Pause and reflect on Israel's history and God's love shown forth by His power over Israel's enemies, time after time after time.

SELAH. Take time now to take it personally. Pause, take time to see Who God is in the midst of all your current trials and turmoil. God is still God. God is still sovereign. God is still on the throne. Nothing throws Him off balance. He is the one Who accurately and justly weighs and measures. He balances and rightly judges those Who violently oppose Him.

Not only has God shown this throughout the ages in His preservation of His people, but He is a God

Who does not change. He is the same yesterday, today, and forever. We can continue to rely on Him always, every time, in every way, to do what is best, good, and right for Israel today, and in our own personal situations as well. SELAH.

Pause, now and turn this gem towards the light so you can see the beauty of it, from another perspective - as it applies more precisely to your own very specific and personal times of distress.

When things seem upside down in your life, when you've received that terrible doctor report about your child, your loved one, or yourself, there's stress. When facing loss, death, or the operating table, there's stress. But the same God Who has the power to make wars to cease (Psalm 46:9), Who, at one word can break a bow and melt the earth, is the same awesome and sovereign God Who lovingly tells His people in Psalm 46:10 to **"be still"**. The floods will not overtake you. The raging seas will not destroy you. He holds you in the palm of His hand, as the apple of His eye. He's protecting you, and He's got you covered in the midst of your trials.

God says to you now, not only to be still, but verse 10 of Psalm 46 says also to "**know**" that He is God. We can have confidence, not in ourselves or in our own man-made systems and devices, but we can put all our confidence and our trust in the Living God Who is God over every detail!

The final "selah" found in Psalm 46 verse 11 affirms to us that God is with us. He is our fortress and refuge. When realizing our own weakness, and seeing His grace and power, we are led to exalt and praise Him. For He alone is our fortress, the God of Yaakov (Jacob), our Mashiach, Savior and Lord.

The Power of the Pause:

The Many Gems of Psalm 118

Psalm 46 has many gems which lead us to bless and exalt God. Psalm 118 also has gems to lead us to bless and exalt God. We just need to take the time to pause and look deeper. There's power displayed in the pauses. Let's pause now to reflect on this power in Psalm 118 verse 17.

Oh Israel, and those who truly know the Lord, you shall not die, but live, and you shall declare His praises, as He has promised.

Again, a key is found in the gem of the pause. So let's not fly over God's Word too quickly, but take time - to pause, to stop, to reflect, to learn, to SELAH - to find the gem.

> *"..YOU SHALL NOT DIE, BUT LIVE, AND YOU SHALL DECLARE HIS PRAISES..." A KEY IS FOUND IN THE GEM OF THE PAUSE.*

The pause may be what God is using in your life now, so you can really live.

Are you ready to take time to really look to Him and live - to pause, to realize the priorities of life, and to declare His praises? It could be that this is your season of life to pause, prioritize, and move forward - to live in His victory – over death!

Will you pause now to reflect on God and his purposes for you - as if your very life depended on it.

SELAH!

7

HIS VICTORY

"*T*he LORD *hath chastened me sore: but he hath not given me over unto death.*" *(Psalm 118:18)*

Oh how we don't love chastening. Mishle 3 (Proverbs 3) verses 11-12 tells us "My son, despise not the chastening of the Lord, for whom the Lord loveth he correcteth..." The Brit Hadasha (New

> OH HOW WE DON'T LOVE CHASTENING...

Testament) contains the book of Hebrews which further describes the use and purpose of chastening in our lives.

Hebrews 12:6-11 says:

"For whom the Lord loveth he chasteneth, and scourgeth every son whom he receiveth.

If ye endure chastening, God dealeth with you as with sons; for what son is he whom the father chasteneth not? But if ye be without chastisement, whereof all are partakers, then are ye bastards, and not sons. Furthermore we have had fathers of our flesh which corrected us, and we gave them reverence: shall we not much rather be in subjection unto the Father of spirits, and live? For they verily for a few days chastened us after their own pleasure; but he **for our profit, that we might be partakers of his holiness. Now no chastening for the present seemeth to be joyous, but grievous: nevertheless afterward it yieldeth the peaceable fruit of righteousness** unto them which are exercised thereby."

Don't let a time of correction or discipline make you bitter, but allow its work to be accomplished so that you become better, not bitter.

> *GOD WILL ALWAYS DO WHAT IS BEST FOR US, TO BRING US BACK TO HIMSELF.*

You may not understand the hard times. You may not like it. But don't give up. It all has its purpose. Our Heavenly Father knows everything and sees what is coming into your life in the years ahead. He knows what is best for you. He knows what will work for you and He knows all that will help you now, and in the long run.

God has all authority. He has triumphed over darkness, destruction, and death. He Who is victorious can give you victory over your most trying challenges.

Though we may think He's making us suffer through devastating circumstances, His promise is that He will never give us more than we can handle. **His promise to us who believe in Him, is that He** is working <u>ALL</u> things together for good.

God's ways are way higher than our ways! What you think is devastating now, could actually be how the all-

> *GOD'S WAYS ARE WAY HIGHER THAN OUR WAYS!*

powerful and omniscient Father is lovingly blessing you. It may not look like much of a blessing. It may be hurtful and painful, but it ultimately may be protecting you from something far more devastating down the road, say for all eternity!

7A

ETERNITY

There indeed is an eternity. Whether you believe it or not, there is. **Unbelief does not nullify the reality of its existence.**

After the physical body of flesh dies, that's not the end. The spirit is eternal.

> *UNBELIEF IN ETERNITY DOES NOT NULLIFY THE REALITY OF ITS EXISTENCE.*

After your physical body dies, that is not the end.

The Hebrew prophet Daniel says, *"And many of*

them that sleep in the dust of the earth shall awake, some to everlasting life, and some to shame and everlasting contempt." (Daniel 12:2)

There are many references to the resurrection in the regular observances and life of the Jewish people. Rabbis have spoken of it, and Scriptures clearly speak of it.

There is a heaven and there is a hell. Hell is the eternal separation from God. Hell is a place of torment and darkness far worse than anything any man can experience during this brief physical life on earth.

Sometimes trials lead us to question our beliefs. Sometimes hardships force us to ask ourselves if there is life after death, if there is a heaven and hell.

If it's all true, and indeed it is, do you know for sure where you will be spending your eternity? You can know beyond a shadow of doubt. Assurance comes by accepting God's truth.

We have been given opportunities in our lives to accept or reject God. Sometimes a time of intense trial and tribulation will be what causes us to grow close to God.

An intense trial may be the impetus for change. Difficult trials may lead to a time of repenting, a time to turn away from what is anti-God and turn towards the one true God.

Perhaps a current trial in your life is causing you to move away from God? Why not allow the trial to move you closer towards Him? Seek God in the midst of your situation. God sees the heart that is seeking Him.

> *HEED GOD'S CALL. BELIEVE GOD'S WORD. IT MEANS THE DIFFERENCE BETWEEN AN ETERNITY WITH HIM, OR, WHEN YOU BREATHE YOUR LAST, AN ETERNITY WITHOUT HIM.*

Perhaps God is using a trial so that your eyes will look to Him, so that you will call on His Name in faith, believing that He, and *only* He, is your Answer. **Believing in Him or not** believing in Him means the difference between an eternity with Him, or, when you breathe your last, an eternity without Him. Don't wait till your own end. Believe God now.

One day you may realize that **even your next breath is His gift to you.** Don't wait until a devastating circumstance strikes your life. **Heed His call now, while He's giving you this opportunity.**

In the Hebrew Scriptures, the prophet Isaiah tells us to: *"Seek ye the LORD while he may be found, call ye upon him while he is near: Let the wicked forsake his way, and the unrighteous man his thoughts: and let him return unto the LORD, and he will have mercy upon him; and to our God, for he will abundantly pardon."* (Isaiah 55:6-7)

Accept God's promise and mercy. Accept His Hope and His victory over all sin and evil. God is able to give you hope to endure anything that you may be facing. Receive His great grace and love, as He draws you to Him through whatever means He chooses.

Allow God to use your times of hardship, or your times of being chastened, or times of being disciplined and loved, as times where you can draw close in the comfort of His arms. The strong arms of your loving Heavenly Father will hold you up. He truly knows best - even when we don't understand it all! The key is to trust Him, continue believing, and to rely on Him through the trials - for ultimate victory.

It could be that you've had rough times where you could say as Psalm 118:18 says "The LORD hath chastened me sore: but he hath not given me over unto death."

In the world there are great tribulations. The tribulations now, and the tribulation ahead that will be coming into the world, will be as refining fires. Through it all, God is our Hope. Heed God's call in your life, and call upon Him now.

8

THE ROAD LESS TRAVELED

*"**O**pen to me the gates of righteousness: I will go into them, and I will praise the LORD: This gate of the LORD, into which the righteous shall enter. I will praise thee: for thou hast heard me, and art become my salvation."* *(Psalm 118:19-21)*

The Hebrew word here for "salvation" is "yshuw'ah". The name also translates as

95

"deliverance", "saving health", "help", "victory", and "prosperity". We can praise God Who has redeemed us, delivered us. He provides help for us, and offers victory for us. Knowing and loving Him brings prosperity to our souls.

As we seek God, He will open up doors for us. The doors He opens, no man can shut. The doors God opens provide water for the thirsty soul. The doors that God opens lead us on paths to know more of Him and His righteousness. It's not that we become perfect in our own righteousness, but that we see His righteousness. In seeing His righteousness, we then can praise Him for Who He is.

When our hearts are open to Him, then through His mercy, He shows us more of Himself. We see all that He has done for us.

When you love someone, you want to spend time with them. If you truly love God, you will desire to be with Him. If you truly love Him, you will desire to spend more time with Him, spend time in

His house, walk in His will, and reflect His good and pure ways. The more you spend time with God, the more you can enjoy the sweetness of His presence. The more time we spend with Him, we, being of Him, become more and more like Him.

These days we don't see many people flocking to worship God, to enter his gates, to enjoy His sweet presence. As the world becomes less tolerant of Biblical faith, more and more people are falling away, far away from Him. **More and more people are choosing to go in the direction of the world's majority - opting to walk through gates of political correctness instead of Biblical truth.**

More and more people are following the popular opinion, going the way of the crowd. It may look like the right way to go because everybody's doing it. Some people think foolishly that the crowd or the majority opinion of the world is the right way. The truth is that the way of the crowd isn't always right. The right way may not be the most popular road to take. The way of the righteous is narrow. Few take the way of truth and righteousness. Few follow what the Scriptures say. Few take the narrow road of righteousness. Those who do follow after God's ways are often rejected and mocked. The way of following God and His righteousness is often the road less traveled.

However, God's truth still stands. No matter what is going on in the world, those who seek God and His righteousness, those who take the narrow

> *GOD HIMSELF BECOMES THE DOOR, THE GATE, WHEREBY WE CAN ENTER INTO HIS PRESENCE.*

road, will find Him. God will open the door for us to enter into His presence. God Himself becomes the door, the gate, whereby we can enter into His righteousness. He makes the way for us and bids us to come to Him. God becomes our salvation.

This is your opportunity to come to Him. The world can have you spinning in many different directions and it offers no real and lasting inner peace.

Ask God to open a door for you today - to show you more of Himself. **Ask G-d to show you what it means when He says that He becomes our "yshuw'ah", our salvation.**

When you ask Him from your heart, He will open up the door of understanding, to discern, with wisdom, the matters of the spirit.

God will open for you the way of victory, and give you a triumphant peace that passes all understanding. He will hear your words. He will hear the cry of your heart, and He will give you the Answer. And you will praise Him for it. He will show you His salvation and the way He has made just for you. So, you will say as it says in Psalm 118 verse 21: *"I will praise thee: for thou hast heard me, and art become my salvation." (in Hebrew, the word used here for salvation is "Yeshua".)*

Today if you are hearing His voice, if you are feeling that God is nudging your spirit, even in the smallest way, to learn more of Him, then don't harden your heart. What the Lord does is marvelous. It is His doing, not my own doing, and not your own doing. **It is God's doing, and it is marvelous in our eyes.**

9

FIRST AS REJECTED SERVANT/THEN AS KING

"The stone which the builders refused is become the head stone of the corner. This is the LORD's doing; it is marvellous in our eyes. This is the day which the LORD hath made; we will rejoice and be glad in it. Save now, I beseech thee, O LORD: O LORD, I beseech thee, send now prosperity. Blessed be he that cometh in the name of the LORD: we have blessed you out

of the house of the LORD." (Psalm 118:22-26)

This is the day the Lord has made for <u>you</u>. God is doing a great work. This great work is connected with the Chief Cornerstone of His building.

The Great Designer:

The Chief Cornerstone

The Psalmist knows whatever the Lord does and builds is marvelous. Maybe God is building now in your life. Perhaps God has been

> *GOD HAS BEEN WEAVING IT ALL TOGETHER... SO THAT YOU MIGHT KNOW HIM BETTER.*

laying a foundation in your life, as a skillful builder and architect. He is the perfect designer. He uses all the various circumstances of your life, the ups, the downs, the "chance" meetings. He uses the new and perhaps sudden change of direction that your life has now taken. God has designed it all. **He's been weaving it all together to make**

something perfect and beautiful in your life, so that you might know Him better.

While God lays the foundation of your life and has put it all together for you, He Himself wants to be your foundation, *the head stone of the corner*. He's the Rock, and has made Himself to be the chief cornerstone, the foundation and creator of all that is.

The Prophet Isais (Isaiah) speaks of the importance of the cornerstone. Isaiah 28:16-17 says: "Therefore thus saith the Lord GOD, Behold, I lay in Zion for a foundation a stone, a tried stone, a precious corner stone, a sure foundation: he that believeth shall not make haste. Judgment also will I lay to the line, and righteousness to the plummet: and the hail shall sweep away the refuge of lies, and the waters shall overflow the hiding place."

This speaks of the Messiah-King who is to be the touchstone of Zion.

The Scripture speaks of a blessing for those who

believe in Him, and also speaks a warning for those who don't trust in Him.

God Himself lays Himself down as our Rock, the foundation of our lives, our salvation, and He is the chief and precious cornerstone upon which He builds into our lives.

Though many reject Him, it doesn't nullify the fact that **He remains the Rock, the Cornerstone, the sure foundation.** He remains. Though scoffers scoff, and mockers mock, He still is Who He is.

Though man tries to build his own tower without God, man will always fail. Though we wrongfully prop ourselves up as the master planner and builder, using our own ways and means to make our own foundation in life, it won't work. **Without God, the plans of man will miserably fail.**

Those who reject God, by building their own lives without Him, will one day come to realize that the very stone they rejected, actually is the only righteous King and ruler over all, the sure foundation.

Not only is God *a* rock, but He is **The** Rock, the one and only Rock. He is our sure foundation in all of life. Though rejected by many, that which is built by God, **where He has laid Himself down as the chief cornerstone**, will remain strong and sturdy. We are blessed in that. We rejoice in that. And in Him we find all prosperity. We will rejoice and be glad in Him Who is our Rock. our Hope and sure foundation.

> *...HE HAS LAID HIMSELF DOWN AS THE CHIEF CORNERSTONE...*

10

THE GREAT SACRIFICE

*"*G*od is the LORD, which hath shewed us light: bind the sacrifice with cords, even unto the horns of the altar." (Psalm 118:27)*

This is a simple declaration of faith. Yes, God is the Lord. He spoke the Word and light came to be. He brings light and hope and comfort into our lives. But what is the meaning of this "sacrifice with cords, even unto the horns of the altar"?

The ancient system of sacrifice involved

bringing an unblemished lamb for sacrifice in the temple. The animal was bound with cords and tied to the horns of the altar in the Holy of Holies.

Through the offering up of the lamb by the High Priest, atonement was made for the sins of the people. As we have learned, a blood sacrifice was required. God accepted this means of atonement, and forgave the people of their sins.

The animal sacrificial system did not permanently cover all sins for all time, but it had to be offered over and over and over again. It was how God set things up for that period of time.

Year after year, on the Hebrew day of Atonement, the Israelites would come from all over and bring their sacrificial offering before the High Priest, who would then offer it up, following the law that God had laid out.

Life Through the Blood Atonement

What did God say to Moses about the blood atonement? **"For the life of the flesh is in the blood: and I have given it to you upon the altar to make an** atonement for your souls: for it is the blood that maketh an atonement for the soul."

"...FOR IT IS THE BLOOD THAT MAKETH ATONEMENT FOR THE SOUL..."

(Leviticus 17:11)

Year after year, the sacrifice had to be made as payment for the penalty of sin. The giving of the sacrifice, as God prescribed it, was accepted by God as payment so that man could be set free from sin's consequences, and from eternal death and separation from God.

The sin nature in man, since the fall of Adam in the garden, causes us to continually miss the mark of perfection.

Decade after decade, century after century since the time Moshe (Moses) had been given the law, though man intently tried to follow the law of Moshe perfectly, man kept falling short. Man realized the need for a sacrifice, one to save from sin. Man realized his need for an atoning work. He realized his own imperfections in the light of the Holy God. He realized his need of a savior. Even with all the good works that man did, and in all the good works that we may do, we can never be perfectly righteous in and of ourselves. We need an atoning work. We, too, need a savior.

> *ONLY A PERFECT SACRIFICE, PRECISELY PRESCRIBED BY GOD, COULD DO THE ATONING WORK.*

Even if we were to sacrifice our very life, and die for a righteous cause, our death could not bring atonement for our sins, nor could our own death bring atonement for anyone else's sins.

Only a perfect sacrifice, precisely prescribed by God, could do the atoning work.

The Redeemer of Israel

In light of all that's been said in Psalm 118 so far, you may have many questions. Have you ever really pondered "Who exactly is the rejected stone?" Have you ever thought "Why is there so much mention of a blood atonement and sacrifice in the Torah?" You may ask, "What do the Scriptures say about the Messiah?" Perhaps you have other questions. The answers are found in the Scriptures, some of which we will review in this first book of your journey.

Torah is God's Divinely inspired word, filled with truth and prophecies. Throughout the pages of Scripture, a coming savior and redeemer of Israel is described.

We will look at some of the Holy Scriptures which give prophetic insights about the Redeemer Messiah.

The book of Genesis records that a time would come when the head of satan would be crushed under the heels of a Redeemer to come. (Genesis 3:15)

Throughout the Torah and the Old Testament Scriptures, there are prophecies concerning this Redeemer to come, the perfect Savior.

Let us look deeper now, at some of the prophecies given by the Jewish prophets of old.

Of the Mashiach/Messiah, the **Hebrew Scriptures** reveal the mystery:

✡ The Messiah would be Jewish, and would come through the line of Abraham, Isaac and Jacob. (Gen 22:18, Gen 21:22 and Gen 28:14)

✡ He would come at a set time (Gen 49:10), and be born in a set place. (Micah 5:2)

✡ He would come before the destruction of Herod's temple in 70 C.E. (Daniel 9:26)

✡ He would be preceded by a messenger sent of God. (Malachi 3:1)

✡ He would have a Divine nature. (Isaiah 9:5-7)

✡ It was prophesied that Messiah would be anointed to teach and he's set captives free. (Isaiah 61:1)

✡ He would be blameless and without guile. (Isaiah 53:9)

✡ And though He would work great miracles (Isaiah 35:5-6), he would be rejected by his own people. (Psalm 69:8)

✡ Messiah would bear the reproach of many. (Psalm 69:9)

✡ And He would be betrayed. (Psalm 41:9)

✡ He would be sold for thirty pieces of silver.

(Zechariah 11:13 prophecy)

✡ He would be smitten. (Micah 5:1)

✡ He would be spit upon and scourged. (Isaiah 50:6)

✡ Messiah would suffer greatly. (Psalm 22:14-15)

> *ONLY A PROPHET INSPIRED BY GOD CAN ACCURATELY SPEAK IN INCREDIBLE DETAIL ABOUT WHAT IS TO COME, GENERATIONS BEFORE IT ACTUALLY COMES TO PASS.*

✡ The prophet Daniel gave an exact time in history, to the day, when this Redeemer, the suffering servant, would be cut off (killed), and the temple destroyed. (Daniel 9:24-26)

Only God knows ALL things, past, present and future. **Only a prophet inspired by God can perfectly and accurately predict in such incredible detail an event to take place hundreds** of years prior to its occurrence.

What redeemer could possibly fill each of these prophecies? Messiah would not fulfill only one aspect, or one prophecy, but has to fulfill ALL given prophecies that all the Jewish prophets have written about in the Holy Scriptures. **Each and every reference has to be 100% accurate for it to be God's prophecy.**

Daniel prophesied that the Redeemer would be "cut off" at a specific time. This cutting off would happen at the specific time of the Passover remembrance in Jerusalem, and it would occur *prior* to the destruction of the Temple in 70 AD.

> *EACH AND EVERY REFERENCE HAS TO BE 100% ACCURATE FOR IT TO BE GOD'S PROPHECY.*

If this event hadn't occurred precisely as Daniel had predicted it, then Daniel would be a false prophet.

To come to accept each detail, prophecy and event given throughout Torah, Tanakh, Ketuvim and all of God's written Word is to come to your breakthrough. It is the key to great freedom and victory in your life.

Passover & Mashiach (Messiah)

As the Psalmist speaks of atonement and sacrifice, we may naturally think of some of the High Holy days of the Jewish faith wherein sacrifices were rendered. One such day is the Spring Holy Day of Passover. Let's consider now the meaning of Passover.

The first Passover came when the Hebrews were in bondage in Egypt, and is detailed in Exodus chapter 12. It was the time when the blood of the sacrificed lamb, was spread over the doorposts of each house. The blood of the innocent lamb on the doorposts was what spared the Hebrews from God's judgment of death. By the sacrifice, and by applying the blood of the lamb on the doorposts, there was freedom from death. Death "passed over" those households that were covered by the blood. This was the first Passover, and the Israelites received freedom from death, and received freedom from Egyptian bondage as well.

This first Passover was symbolic of an even greater Passover to come. The prophet Isaiah spoke of a Redeemer who would be "cut off". This would occur, as we now know, during the time of the Jewish Passover. The Redeemer was "cut off", killed, sacrificed as God's Passover Lamb for us. It happened in the exact timing of days, weeks and years, as was accurately prophesied hundreds of years prior by the Jewish prophets of God.

Torah and the Hebrew Scriptures are filled with many prophecies. Throughout God's Word is the plan of atonement. As in ancient days, atonement had to come through the shedding of innocent blood. Torah is filled with many prophecies concerning the Messiah. In all of history, there is only one who perfectly fulfills all that the prophets have spoken about. It is Mashiach/ Messiah who IS.

There is only one who made a great sacrifice, in one perfect and final atonement. It is the perfect one Who comes as Redeemer and Savior. **He is Jewish**, born into a Jewish family, in a Jewish city, in a Jewish culture. He attended synagogue, and kept all Jewish laws perfectly. **Through his suffering, redemption would come.** As the Hebrew prophet Daniel said in Isaiah 53, the Redeemer comes as a "suffering servant", and through suffering would bring victory for the world.

This **Passover Lamb of God, through the shedding of His blood, and applying it through faith on to the doorposts of our hearts, gives us freedom and life,** and brings us salvation from eternal

> *THROUGH HIS SUFFERING, REDEMPTION WOULD COME.*

punishment and death. **The answer is found in the meaning of His given Hebrew name meaning "Salvation".**

This sacrifice was very different from past sacrifices, in that the shedding of *this* blood was the blood of one who was totally pure, and totally righteous, and totally

> *APPLYING THE BLOOD OF THIS PASSOVER LAMB OF GOD, THROUGH FAITH, ONTO THE DOORPOSTS OF OUR HEARTS, GIVES US FREEEDOM AND LIFE.*

without fault. He was the God-given Lamb without blemish, fulfilling the requirements of the Law. It was the only qualified perfect sacrifice that would be accepted once and for all.

No other sacrifice could <u>perfectly</u> atone to make it a sufficient one-time sacrifice to cover and **atone for all eternity.** Only one perfect sacrifice could qualify to meet God's perfect standard of purity and righteousness <u>for all time</u>. It had to be of God Himself.

The only perfect, totally pure and blameless one who could ever offer the perfect and final atonement once and for all, to adequately atone

for the sins of all mankind, would be from the very throne of G-d. He would come to show His great love for us, by giving of Himself for us. There could be no other way. Any other way falls short of the requirement for purity and perfection. God's way satisfies the perfect requirements of the perfect and Holy God. God alone is perfect. It is the only final and permanent way. It is the perfect, holy, and final atonement needed.

The sacrifices made by man were all pointing to, and leading up to the one great and final atoning work of God Himself. The sacrifice of God, Who gave HIS Passover Lamb, was able to accomplish what man, in man's imperfection, could never do. The prophets spoke of this.

And who is it who spoke *through* the Hebrew prophets? **Was it not G-d Who spoke through the Hebrew prophets** of the Tanakh?

The Prophets Spoke of the Coming Messiah

In Jewish tradition, the Passover Seder,

especially the 8th day, is very much connected to the Messiah. There is symbolism, and anticipation, hoping and waiting for Messiah to come.

What do the Scriptures and Jewish prophets specifically say about the *coming* of Messiah?

✡ The Jewish prophet Isaiah said that this Savior of all the world would be a rod out of the stem of Jesse. (Isaiah 11:1,2)

✡ In Genesis, it is written that Messiah would be of the seed of Jacob. (Genesis 28:13,14; Numbers 24:17,19)

✡ Messiah would be born a king in the line of David. (Isaiah 9:7, 2Samuel 7:12,13, Jeremiah 23:5, 30:9)

✡ Salvation would come through one of the tribe of Judah. (Genesis 49:8-10, Micah 5:2)

✡ Messiah would be born of the seed of Isaac.

(Genesis 17:19, 21:12, 26:2-4)

✡ Messiah would be born of the seed of Abraham. (Genesis 17:7,8; 26:3-4)

✡ The Hebrew prophet Micah, gave the place of Messiah's birth. Messiah would be born specifically in Bethlehem. (Micah 5:2)

Salvation through Messiah comes to the world from our Heavenly Father. While we were still sinners, straying away as lost imperfect sheep, He came for us

> ONE FINAL ATONEMENT FOR ALL WHO WOULD BELIEVE WOULD BE THE FULFILLMENT OF ALL PROPHECIES IN THE HEBREW SCRIPTURES...

to offer Himself as the perfect Passover Lamb to meet His own requirement for righteousness, to pay the penalty for our sins, so that we can be united in love, and with Him for all eternity.

Just as Psalm 118 indicates, God is the Lord and

He has shown us light, even through sacrifice, even on the altar of suffering.

There would be the one final atonement for all who would believe. It would be the fulfillment of all prophecies in the Hebrew writings, and would be what each of the Hebrew feasts in Torah ultimately point to. It would be the only pure, perfect and therefore, final sacrifice needed.

Only one person fulfills each and every prophecy given by the Hebrew prophets. Only one Messiah was born of the seed of Abraham, born of the seed of Isaac, of the

ONLY ONE PERSON FULFILLS EACH AND EVERY PROPHECY GIVEN BY THE HEBREW PROPHETS... ONLY ONE MESSIAH FULFILLED THESE PROPHECIES WITH 100% ACCURACY...

tribe of Judah, in the line of David, of the seed of Jacob, a rod out of the stem of Jesse, was Jewish, and would come through the line of Abraham, Isaac and Jacob, coming at a set time be born in a set place (Micah 5:2), be preceded by a messenger sent of God, would come riding humbly on a donkey, would be anointed to teach, be blameless and without guile, would work great miracles, would be rejected by his own people, would bear the reproach of many, would be betrayed, would be sold for thirty pieces of silver, would be smitten, would be spit upon and scourged, would suffer greatly, would be cut off (killed), and the temple destroyed.

So do you believe the Torah writings, and the prophets Isaiah, Micah, Malachi, Ezekiel, Daniel, and Jeremiah who boldly spoke as God had led them?

Only God knows ALL things, past, present and future. **Only a prophet inspired by God can accurately speak in incredible detail what is to come, generations before it actually comes to pass.** We are a people blessed to see the fulfillment now.

The Redeemer, as the prophets foretold, came once as a righteous and victorious humble servant, and will come again as a righteous and victorious king to rule and to reign over all the earth, in great triumph. **Mashiach is coming soon as King!** We look forward to His coming. As prophesied, **His first coming was as a suffering servant, but His second coming will be as victorious King for all eternity.**

The Hebrew prophet, Zechariah, told the Daughter of Zion to rejoice. Zechariah knew that her king would come to her, **righteous, and just, having salvation, coming lowly, humbly and riding on a donkey.** (See Zechariah 9:9)

There is only One who fulfills it all. His very name

> *HIS VERY NAME MEANS "SALVATION".*

means salvation. "Yeshua" in Hebrew means "salvation". It is the Hebrew name given to the Redeemer. Yeshua is Israel's Hope and our Salvation. Jesus (the English version of the name Yeshua) was Jewish. His given name was the Hebrew name, Yeshua. His birth name was Yeshua. **He was Jewish, born of Jewish parents.**

Only Yeshua/Jesus fulfills each of the hundreds of prophecies to perfection. He is the Atonement needed, the One spoken of by the prophets. He is the King of kings, and the glory of Israel.

The prophet Isaiah spoke of a great miraculous sign that God would give for us: "Therefore the Lord himself shall give you a sign; **Behold, a virgin shall conceive, and bear a son, and shall call his name Immanuel.**" (literally "God with us") (Isaiah 7:14)

Who has fulfilled each of these prophecies of Torah, of the Scripture writings?

Do the research. Search out the Scriptures. Look for Truth. Pray to Adonai to reveal it to you, and He will.

> *SEARCH OUT THE SCRIPTURES. LOOK FOR TRUTH. PRAY TO ADONAI TO REVEAL IT TO YOU, AND HE WILL.*

Solomon, in the Proverbs says: "**It is the glory of God to conceal a thing: but the honour of kings is to search out a matter.**" (Proverbs 25:11). So, search it out. Seek and find it.

Many will oppose. Many will fight it. But in the end, there is Truth, and God will bring insight, revelation, and victory for His chosen, for His beloved Israel.

The Truth is found in God's Word. Torah speaks about the priority of God and His written Word. God's Word takes priority over all else. The issue is: Are you believing in God's written Word, and

> *THE ISSUE IS: ARE YOU BELIEVING IN GOD'S WRITTEN WORD, AND DO YOU BELIEVE WHAT THE JEWISH PROPHETS OF THE OLD TESTAMENT HAVE DECLARED ABOUT MESSIAH?*

staying true to God's written Scripture? What do you say about each of the prophecies concerning Messiah? If you believe God's written Word, do you believe God's written word and prophecies given through the Jewish prophets of the Tanakh (Old Testament) - Isaiah, Jeremiah, Ezekiel, Daniel? Are you true to God's Word throughout Tanakh, or true to something else? Do you believe in the Jewish Messiah spoken of by the prophets?

In the end, the mystery will unfold, eyes will see it, and all will bow in humble adoration of the One King, Perfect Redeemer, Lord over all. This is another prophecy that will prove true at God's appointed time in the future. His reign will be forever.

"Of the increase of his government and peace there shall be no end, upon the throne of David, and upon his kingdom, to order it, and to establish it with judgement and justice from henceforth even for ever." (Isaiah 9:7)

The One Pierced

Zechariah 14 states: **"For I will gather all nations against Jerusalem to battle;** and the city shall be taken, and the houses rifled, and the women ravished; and half of the city shall go forth into captivity, and the residue of the people shall not be cut off from the city. **Then shall the LORD go forth, and fight against those nations,** as when he fought in the day of battle. **And his feet shall stand in that day upon the mount of Olives, which is before** Jerusalem on the east, and the mount of Olives shall cleave in the midst thereof toward the east and toward the west, and there shall be a very great

> *"...AND I WILL POUR UPON THE HOUSE OF DAVID, AND UPON THE INHABITANTS OF JERUSALEM, THE SPIRIT OF GRACE AND OF SUPPLICATIONS: AND THEY SHALL LOOK UPON ME WHOM THEY HAVE PIERCED, AND THEY SHALL MOURN FOR HIM, AS ONE MOURNETH FOR HIS ONLY SON..."*

valley; and half of the mountain shall remove toward the north, and half of it toward the south. And ye shall flee to the valley of the mountains.. and the LORD my God shall come, and all the saints with thee... And the LORD shall be king over all the earth: in that day shall there be one LORD, and his name one." (ref: Zechariah 14:2-5,9)

There is a day coming, that the prophet Zechariah foretells: "... And I will pour upon the house of David, and upon the inhabitants of Jerusalem, the spirit of grace and of supplications: and they shall look upon me whom they have pierced, and they shall mourn for him, as one mourneth for his only son, and shall be in bitterness for him, as one that is in bitterness for his firstborn." (Zechariah 12:9b-10)

Who is the one who will pour out His grace on the house of David, who also says they "shall look upon **me** whom they have **pierced**"?

The day will come when each will stand before God. We will give account for what we have heard and what we know, what we have accepted and what we have rejected.

> *ASK GOD TO SHOW YOU WHAT IT MEANS WHEN HE SAYS THAT HE BECOMES OUR "YSHUW'AH", OUR SALVATION.*

A day will come when we shall look upon Him Whom we have pierced.

The one pierced is the one Who, in His love, has made atonement for us. He has become the Sacrificial Lamb. Wounded and pierced, yet victorious. He has become our Salvation. His nail-pierced hands and nail-pierced feet, and His death on the cross meant atonement, and our salvation. His Resurrection over death shows us His victory over death and sin.

Time after time, God gives us opportunity to know Him, to call out to Him. He offers Himself to those who would believe. He invites us, His beloved, to share in His love, in His triumph and to rule victoriously with Him.

He is the One Who loved you so much that He was willing to die for you, to give you His all, His most precious life -- for you. By doing this, by making atonement, He makes the way for you, His beloved, to be with Him forever, for all eternity.

> *IT'S THE MOST BEAUTIFUL LOVE STORY EVER WRITTEN...*

It's the most beautiful love story ever written. It's Torah. It's His Holy Scriptures. It's all that the prophets have declared. It's the Bible. It is God's full plan of redemption, His inspired Word, written for you, and it is Truth.

11

THE SONG OF THE BELOVED

"Thou art my God, and I will praise thee: thou art my God, I will exalt thee." (Psalm 118:28)

In the Song of Solomon (6:3), it says "I am my beloved's and my beloved is mine". In Hebrew, it's "ani l dodi v dodi li". It's used a lot at Hebrew weddings, and symbolizes a deep love and committed relationship between the lover and his beloved. **The relationship that God offers with you, His chosen and His beloved, is meant to be more beautiful, deeper and richer than any relationship you have ever had.**

Human love, though one may strive to work at loving perfectly, could never be perfect. Man's love due to man's sin nature will disappoint and fall short, sometimes far short, and sometimes brutally short.

> *THE RELATIONSHIP GOD OFFERS YOU IS MORE BEAUTIFUL, DEEPER AND RICHER THAN ANY RELATIONSHIP YOU HAVE EVER HAD.*

However, **the love of God Who is perfect, is a perfect love.** God's love is the highest and purest and deepest love there is.

G-d offers this love for you now. Not only does He offer us His love, but He allows you to call Him yours. We are His, He is ours. **It's personal.**

So, take it personally. "ani l dodi v dodi li". "I am my beloved's and my beloved is mine". He meant it to be personal, since the beginning of time. It's a relationship that He longs for us to enter into with Him.

It's a personal relationship with our God Who made every fiber of our being, Who knows us well, Who loves us deeply with <u>perfect</u> love.

Those who can call upon Him now, and say yes to His call, can say as the Psalmist says **"Thou art my God"**. Not in an impersonal way, but in a deeply loving and personal way, you can say "my" God.

He is yours, and you are His. **He is personal, loving, living, and He is with you every moment.**

"Therefore the Lord himself shall give you a sign; **Behold, a virgin shall conceive, and bear a son, and shall call his name Immanuel.**" (Isaiah 7:14)

He is "Immanuel". "Immanuel" is a Hebrew word meaning "God with us". He is with us. He is our Beloved and we are His. He is your God and worthy of all your praises. As it says in Psalm 118:28, *"Thou art <u>my</u> God, and I will praise thee: thou art <u>my</u> God, I will exalt thee."*

Moses heard God's voice and knew God in a personal way. Abraham, also, knew the covenant relationship with God, and was called a friend of God. Isaiah, Jeremiah and prophets called upon God and knew His ways. The prophet Hosea spoke of a day coming that His people will call to Him as His beloved.

"I will betroth thee unto me for ever; yea, I will betroth thee unto me in righteousness, and in judgment, and in lovingkindness, and in mercies. And **I will even betroth thee unto me in faithfulness, and thou shalt know the Lord."** (Hosea 2:19-20)

The only True and Living God is a personal

God. He has been drawing you, and calling you, personally. Answer His call in your life today. Make it personal by responding to His call.

As we near the end of this book, this part of your journey, perhaps you'd like to heed the call of God on your life. In light of all that has been shared here, and in light of God's Word through Torah, and through His prophets in the Holy Scriptures, you have maybe been challenged to respond to Isaiah's words to *"Seek ye the LORD while he may be found, call ye upon him while he is near: Let the wicked forsake his way, and the unrighteous man his thoughts: and let him return unto the LORD, and he will have mercy upon him; and to our God, for he will abundantly pardon."* (Isaiah 55:6-7)

I exhort you to truly seek the Lord, and personally call upon God. As Isaiah said, we should repent of our sin and unrighteousness. When we seek Him, in sincere remorse and repentance of the sins we've committed, He will hear. When we turn to Him, believing Who He is, and trusting in His righteousness, in His atoning Sacrifice, we have His promise that He will indeed have mercy on us. He will not only pardon, but as the prophet Isaiah says he will *abundantly* pardon.

12

A NEW BEGINNING

"O give thanks unto the LORD; for he is good: for his mercy endureth for ever." *(Psalm 118:29)*

Are you giving thanks to the Lord today? Are you thankful to the God of Abraham, Isaac and Jacob - the one true God Who has been so merciful towards you? Can you say that you really love Him with all your heart, soul and might?

Torah clearly declares that there is only one God. The Lord is one. There is only one God in all the earth, and that is the God of Abraham, Isaac, and Jacob. **You are called, as it says in Deuteronomy to love the Lord your God with all your heart with all your soul and to love Him with all your might.**

"And thou shalt love the LORD thy God with all thine heart, and with all thy soul, and with all thy might." (Deuteronomy 6:5)

You can overflow with awe and love towards Him, as you look at God's holiness, His goodness and great mercy. God's loving work brings you salvation. God has graciously given us all we need through His Atonement. His Atonement allows us to enter into His presence for all eternity. One atoning work given for us through His mercy, for us, for all eternity. His great love for us, allows us to love Him. We can love because He first loved us.

How will you respond to God? It's a matter of repentance, faith and trust. We are given the opportunity to repent, turn from where we've been, turn from what hasn't worked. Turn from sin and turn from trusting in other gods, and turn towards the One and only God. Turn to His Word and Truth.

Look to God. He will give you all you need to embrace His great mercy and love. God will even give you the faith and trust to move forward, as you look to Him.

The Gifts of Emunah (Faith) & Bitachon (Trust)

"Emunah" is the Hebrew word for faith. It's found in Bereshit (Genesis) in Chapter 15, verse 6. Abraham had emunah (faith) and <u>believed</u> in the Lord and in His promises, even though Abraham may not have understood at the time how exactly the promise was to be fulfilled. He believed God, and God counted it to Abraham as righteousness.

"And he brought him forth abroad, and said, Look now toward heaven, and tell the stars, if thou be able to number them: and he said unto him, So shall thy seed be. And he believed (emunah, faith) in the LORD; and he counted it to him for righteousness. (Genesis 15:5-6)

Emunah is faith that believes that God is Who He says He is. It is faith that God is in control of all details. It is faith that God is omniscient, all-knowing, and that He can do anything. Nothing is impossible for God.

Are you ready to take a step, like Abraham did, and put your faith in God today? Do you have faith in the authority of God's Word? Do you accept that God's Word is true? Put your faith and trust in the authority of God's Word - that God's Word is what it says it is.

Inherent in the aspect of faith and trust is the fact that we won't fully comprehend it all. Faith and trust are not qualities that we can manufacture on our own. Faith and trust do not come about by our working hard at it, or by man's superior intellect.

The amazing thing about faith and trust is that they are gifts from God. In God's mercy, He gives us the gifts of faith and trust. We are not to put our trust in our own understanding. We are not to put our faith in our own faith. We are to put our trust **in God**. Again, God has to be front and central, first and foremost. Our victory comes when our focus and trust is in Him!

In the book of Proverbs, it is written: **"Trust in the LORD with all thine heart; and lean not unto thine own understanding. In all thy ways acknowledge him, and he shall direct thy paths. Be not wise in thine own eyes: fear the LORD, and depart from evil."** (Proverbs 3:5-7)

The Hebrew word used here for "Trust" is "Bitachon". Bitachon (trust) carries with it the idea of secure and bold confidence, hope, without care or worry. It is trusting in God's mercy and the lovingkindness that He has for you.

Only God can carry away your heavy burdens. You can trust that through His atoning work that He can carry away all your sins (past, present and future). You can trust His great love for you.

You can trust in God's ability to do all He said He will do in the Scriptures, and all that He's spoken through the Hebrew prophets. You can trust in God's great care for you. He loves you so much that He made the Atonement, the provision of the Sacrificial Lamb.

We can take all of our heavy burdens and sins and bring them to God. We can take all the ways we fall short of God's perfection, and give it all to God. He wants us to come to Him and to <u>trust</u> that He's already made the way. He has made the way for us to enter into the holiness of His presence. God is able to forgive you.

It is because of God's mercy, that He gives us

the gifts of faith and trust. What amazing grace and amazing mercy that is! God not only makes the way for us through Atonement, but also gives us what we need to embrace it!

God gives us the faith and trust. It's all God. It's all Him and not of us. There is nothing that we can do to earn it or be worthy of it. God, in His mercy, does it all for us! Forgiveness is a gift. Faith is a gift. Trust is a gift. He gives it all for <u>you</u>.

It is because of God's goodness and mercy that God then counts our faith in Him as righteousness, as He did for Abraham.

Abraham's faith was counted to him as righteousness. God's promise and covenant with Abraham is fulfilled, and blessings for the world have come through this, just as God said. **Through Abraham, and Abraham's seed, the world *is* blessed.**

Do you trust God today? Have you called on

Him in faith? Do you believe His Word and His promises for your life? Bring your questions and concerns to God. He hears and will answer.

If you haven't done so already, call on God today. He will answer you. Pour out your heart to Him, as you would pour out your heart to your closest and trusted loved one.

Remember He is your perfect Father, your perfect Redeemer, Who loves with His perfect love.

Allow God to show Himself to you.

Begin afresh and begin anew today, no matter what your past has been. Make a change, repent from wrongdoing. **Realize that sin separates you from God, but God in His great show of mercy, through His great work of atonement - by His great gift of love - has made a way for you to draw close to Him.**

When I began writing this book, I stated that

you are alive today and that you have a purpose.

You've read Torah, God's Word and you have read in this book what God has spoken through Moses, Isaiah, Ezekiel, Daniel, Micah, David, Jeremiah, and Zechariah, His prophets.

Moses and the prophets said that Messiah would come and suffer and that He would

SIN SEPARATES YOU FROM GOD, BUT GOD, THROUGH HIS GREAT WORK OF ATONEMENT - BY HIS GREAT GIFT OF LOVE - HAS MADE A WAY FOR YOU TO DRAW CLOSE TO HIM. ACCEPT HIS GIFT OF LOVE AND MERCY TODAY.

be First Fruits of those who would rise from the dead, and that He would be a Light for the Jewish people, and a Light for the Gentiles.

Look to the Holy Scriptures yourself, and examine the gems of God's Word further. **Your purpose here on earth, and the purpose of the Jewish people, in these days and in the trying** times ahead, is found in God, in God's Word, His Truth, found in Torah and throughout the Scriptures.

This is your time now to move forward in life, and learn your true purpose in God, and allow Him to do a great work through you.

God appoints times and seasons. God knows everything. You aren't here by chance or accident. God knows every detail of your life. God knows what you are reading now, and all that you are thinking at this very moment. He knows the number of your days.

God has given you life and breath to live this very day. This is an appointed time for you to respond to God. He has given you this day. He has given you His Word. He has given you His Scriptures. He offers you life in Him. He offers His Atonement, His Salvation.

God gives you this opportunity for a NEW BEGINNING, a NEW THING. God offers you now

NEW LIFE in Him. Start now. Take an important step now to acknowledge Him. Receive by faith the great love and mercy that He has for you. Then you will be able, by His loving grace and mercy, to arise to your high calling!

Find your life's calling and your purpose **in Him,** your Beloved Savior.

Pause now. Consider deeply the very detailed prophecies given in Scripture regarding Messiah, God's perfect Sacrificial Lamb, the final atonement needed. Then in <u>faith</u> believe, and <u>trust</u> in God and His atoning work of mercy. Give your heart to Him today. Allow Him to fill you, to be your God, and to bless you now and forever. Then share His message of love.

"Then will I sprinkle clean water upon you, and ye shall be clean: from all your filthiness, and from all your idols, will I cleanse you. **A new heart** also will I give you, and a new spirit will I put within you: and I will take away the stony heart out of your flesh, and I will give you an heart of flesh. And I will put my spirit within you, and cause you to walk in my statutes, and ye shall keep my judgements, and do them. And ye shall dwell in the land that I gave to your fathers; and ye shall be my people, and I will be your God." (Ezekiel 36:25-28)

O give thanks unto the LORD; for he is good: for his mercy endures forever! Let the house of Aaron say it!

HEAR GOD'S WORD IN PSALM 118

"**O** give thanks unto the LORD; for he is good: because his mercy endureth for ever. Let Israel now say, that his mercy endureth for ever. Let the house of Aaron now say, that his mercy endureth for ever. Let them now that fear the LORD say, that his mercy endureth for ever.

I called upon the LORD in distress: the LORD answered me, and set me in a large place. The LORD is on my side; I will not fear: what can man do unto me? The LORD taketh my part with them that help me: therefore shall I see my desire upon them that hate me.

It is better to trust in the LORD than to put confidence in man. It is better to trust in the LORD than to put confidence in princes.

All nations compassed me about: but in the name of the LORD will I destroy them. They compassed me about; yea, they compassed me about: but in the name of the LORD I will destroy them. They compassed me about like bees: they are quenched as the fire of thorns: for in the name of the LORD I will destroy them. Thou hast thrust sore at me that I might fall: but the LORD helped me. The LORD is my strength and song, and is become my salvation.

The voice of rejoicing and salvation is in the tabernacles of the righteous: the right hand of the LORD doeth valiantly. The right hand of the LORD is exalted: the right hand of the LORD doeth valiantly.

I shall not die, but live, and declare the works of the LORD.

The LORD hath chastened me sore: but he hath not given me over unto death.

Open to me the gates of righteousness: I will go into them, and I will praise the LORD: This gate of the LORD, into which the righteous shall enter. I will praise thee: for thou hast heard me, and art become my salvation.

The stone which the builders refused is become the head stone of the corner. This is the LORD's doing; it is marvellous in our eyes. This is the day which the LORD hath made; we will rejoice and be glad in it. Save now, I beseech thee, O LORD: O LORD, I beseech thee, send now prosperity. Blessed be he that cometh in the name of the LORD: we have blessed you out of the house of the LORD.

God is the LORD, which hath shewed us light: bind the sacrifice with cords, even unto the horns of the altar.

Thou art my God, and I will praise thee: thou art my God, I will exalt thee.

O give thanks unto the LORD; for he is good:

for his mercy endureth for ever."

(Psalm 118:1-29)

A CALL TO ARISE

"*A*rise, shine; for thy light is come, and the glory of the LORD is risen upon thee.

For, behold, the darkness shall cover the earth, and gross darkness the people: but the LORD shall arise upon thee, and his glory shall be seen upon thee.

And the Gentiles shall come to thy light, and kings to the brightness of thy rising."

(Isaiah 60:1-3)

Mashiach (Messiah) is the Light Who brings light, eternal salvation, and life for the Jewish people, and also, by grace, to the Gentiles. The Lord is the glory of His beloved Israel.

"The people that walked in darkness have
seen a great light: they that dwell in the land of
the shadow of death, upon them hath the light
shined." *(Isaiah 9:2-3)*

The Torah, Nevtim, Kethuvim (Tanakh / Old
Testament) and the Brit Chadasha (New Covenant)
show the heart of God for you. His Word is His
personal love letter to you, to be searched out and
found by you. Only God can bring Light into our
darkness, and shine Life in the shadows of death.

It is G-d Who opens your heart to search out a
matter. If you ask Him, with an open heart, He will
show Himself strong to you. He will explain hidden
mysteries, age-old prophecies, and bring you to
your rightful place, if you acknowledge His rightful
place in your heart and life.

Psalm 14:1 tells us that **"The fool hath said in
his heart, There is no God."**

The Hebrew prophet Isaias (Isaiah) wrote of a
Righteous One who by his knowledge would justify

many, and bear your iniquities, and make intercession for you. **Those who are wise will seek Him**, and by the grace of G-d, will come to know Him in His fullness.

May you come to know the Messiah.

Proverbs 30:4: **"Who hath ascended up into heaven, or descended? who hath gathered the wind in his fists? who hath bound the waters in a garment? who hath established all the ends of the earth? what is his name, and what is his son's name, if thou canst tell?"**

What is His son's name?

Study the words of the Psalmist: **"I will declare the decree: The Lord hath said unto me, Thou art my Son, this day have I begotten thee... Be wise now therefore, O ye kings: be instructed, ye judges of the earth. Serve the Lord with fear, and rejoice with trembling. Kiss the Son, lest he be angry, and ye perish from the way, when his wrath is kindled but a little. Blessed are they that**

put their trust in him." (Psalm 2:7,10-12)

This day I declare His praises to you, dear reader, and I say indeed blessed are they that put their trust in Him.

Over 100 prophecies from the Old Testament regarding Messiah have been already fulfilled with precise accuracy.

As foretold, your Messiah has come to set you free, to redeem you.

As foretold, He is coming again, in majesty and power, to deliver Israel and to establish His reign as King over all the earth and for all eternity.

It is my prayer that you come to truly know your Messiah, the Redeemer and Hope of Israel.

SOMETHING TO PONDER:

Rav Shaul (the apostle Paul, a Jewish rabbi, taught by rabbi Gamaliel and then by the Rabbi of all rabbis.) writes in the Brit Hadasha: "For scarcely for a righteous man will one die: yet peradventure for a good man some would even dare to die. But God commendeth his love toward us, in that, while we were yet sinners, Christ died for us." (Romans 5:7-8)

Jochanan (John, the Jewish disciple of Yeshua/Jesus also Jewish) says **"In this was manifested the love of God toward us, because that God sent his only begotten Son into the world, that we might live through him. Herein is love, not that we loved God, but that he loved us, and sent his Son to be the propitiation for our sins."** (1 John 4:9-10)

"For as by one man's disobedience many were

made sinners, so by the obedience of one shall many be made righteous." (Romans 5:19)

Shimon Cephas (Aramaic name for the Jewish apostle Simon Peter, disciple of Yeshua/Jesus) wrote: "But ye are a chosen generation, a royal priesthood, an holy nation, a peculiar people; that ye should shew forth the praises of him who hath called you out of darkness into his marvellous light." (1Peter 2:9)

A WORD ABOUT... MESSIAH!

"But thou, Bethlehem Ephratah, though thou be little among the thousands of Judah, yet out of thee shall he come forth unto me that is to be ruler of Israel; whose goings forth have been from old, from everlasting."   Tanakh, Micah 5:2

A WORD ABOUT... YOU!

"For I know the thoughts that I think toward you, saith the LORD, thoughts of peace, and not of evil, to give you an expected end. Then shall ye call upon me, and ye shall go and pray unto me, and I will hearken unto you. **And ye shall seek me, and find me, when ye shall search for me with all your heart. And I will be found of you, saith the LORD: and I will turn away your captivity, and I will gather you from all the nations, and from all the**

places whither I have driven you, saith the LORD; and I will bring you again into the place whence I caused you to be carried away captive."

Jeremiah 29:11-14

Notes about the Text

This first book of The "Series of Seven" is Scripture-based, using Scripture to explain Scripture. Though other works and references, including rabbinic and Talmudic commentaries, may be explored in future writings, we're starting off here with the foundational truths found in the Divinely-inspired Word of God.

Keeping first things first, by establishing a solid foundation in God's Word alone, in the Holy Scriptures, is where your strongest foundation for your NEW LIFE begins!

"So shall my word be that goeth forth out of my mouth: it shall not return unto me void, but it shall accomplish that which I please, and it shall prosper in the thing whereto I sent it." (God's Word through the prophet Isaiah) Isaiah 55:11

A SPECIAL NOTE OF THANKS:

In loving remembrance of my mom and dad who always taught me to have a deep love for God, and a deep love for the Jewish people. With special thanks also to family, friends, and pastors, each of whom have helped me, in various ways, to grow more and more in love with God, and who have stuck with me through thick and thin. In appreciation for the Messianic and rabbinic teaching, and opportunities for service that I've been given over the years. And most importantly, thanks be to God, for His grace and mercy, Who alone gives true Life!

Thankful also for the many relationships God forged years ago in my life, unknown to me at the time that the bonds and blessings would continue to grow and flourish throughout the years, to reach His purpose as it is in these days – but God knew!

"Come, and let us return unto the Lord: for he hath torn, and he will heal us; he hath smitten, and he will bind us up. After two days will he revive us: in the third day he will raise us up, and we shall live in his sight. Then shall we know, if we follow on to know the Lord: his going forth is prepared as the morning; and he shall come unto us as the rain, as the latter and former rain unto the earth."

Hosea 6:1-3

"And ye shall seek me, and find me, when ye shall search for me with all your heart."

Jeremiah 29:13

A WORD ABOUT THE AUTHOR

Carol Scheitlin is a lover of the One True and Living G-d, and has dedicated her life to the One Who has given all life. She has a strong love for Israel, and a lifelong love for the Jewish people, the people chosen of G-d, and through whom Messiah has come. She's served short term in various locations around the world, served long term working in large corporate settings and in small businesses, and for many years served as director of a worldwide ministry outreach. She has a strong work ethic, a desire to serve "as unto the Lord", and G-d continues to open up new doors and new opportunities of service. Adonai has propelled her, at times through great trials of refining, for His glory, to be where she is today. Joyfully, still being refined. May God have all the praise. **His mercies endure forever.** Let the house of Aaron say it.